The Architecture of
PHILIPPE STARCK

FRANCO BERTONI

THE ARCHITECTURE OF
PHILIPPE STARCK

ACADEMY EDITIONS

First published in Great Britain in 1994 by
ACADEMY EDITIONS
An imprint of the Academy Group Ltd

ACADEMY GROUP LTD
42 Leinster Gardens London W2 3AN
Member of VCH Publishing Group

ISBN 1 85490 378 0

Distributed to the trade in the United States of America by
ST MARTINS PRESS
175 Fifth Avenue New York NY 10010

Designer: Auro Lecci
Typesetter: Linograf
Originator: Alfacolor, Chiaroscuro
Printer: Milanostampa

CONTENTS

Franco Bertoni

7   The *architecture à penser* of Philippe Starck

The Architecture of Philippe Starck

49   Les Bains-Douches Night Club
50   L'Élysée Presidential Apartments
52   Café Costes
57   Project for Multipurpose Room, Musée Des Arts Décoratifs
58   Project for Cartier Golden Bridge
59   Musée des Monuments Français, 'Art et Industrie' Exhibition
60   Project for Mercedes-Benz Headquarters
62   Manin Restaurant
68   Project for Starck's First House 'Le Moulin a Vent'
70   Maison Lemoult 'Le Sphinx'
76   Competition Entry for the Tokyo Opera House
80   La Cigale Concert Hall
84   Project for the 'Moon Dog' House
90   Laguiole Knife Factory
94   Café Mystique
98   Royalton Hotel
106   Asahi 'La Flamme'
118   Multipurpose Building 'Nani Nani'
128   Salone Coppola
134   Teatriz Restaurant
149   French Pavilion at the Venice Biennale
156   'Le Baron Vert' Office Building
166   Paramount Hotel
176   Project for the École des Beaux Arts
185   Project for Villa Placido Arango
186   Project for a Pavilion, Groningen Museum of Modern Art
188   Hugo Boss Boutique
192   'La rue Starck'
196   Project for Starck's Second House
197   'The Angle'
198   474 and 6 Cubes
199   Toar
204   Project for Elements of Street Furniture
208   Project for the École Nationale Supérieure des Arts Décoratifs
216   Project for Control Tower, Bordeaux-Merignac Airport
218   Prefabricated House for '3 Suisses'

222   Awards and Exhibitions
223   Bibliography

Among those whom I would like to thank for their collaboration are: Rosanese Luciano for his close involvement and precious advice throughout the project; Arturo del Panta Cristiani; the Parisian friends Nino Pasi and Davide Cappellini; Rosanna La Rocca and Gabriella Greco who have co-ordinated the editorial work.

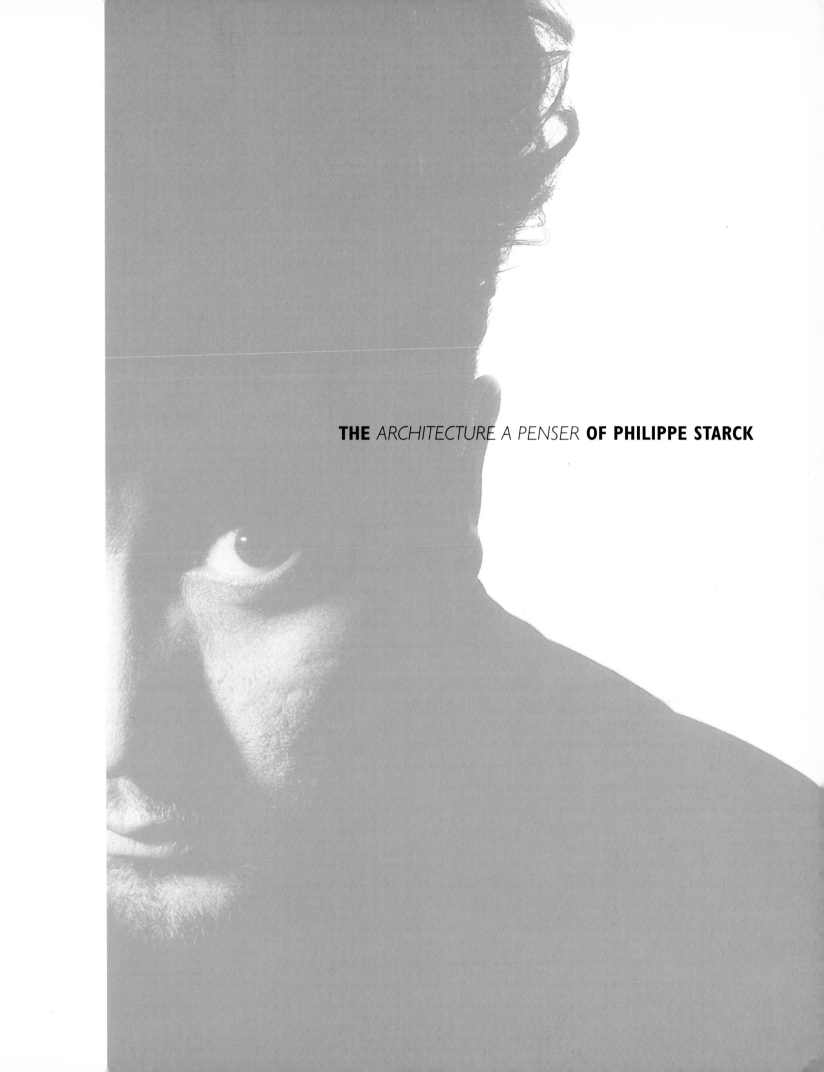

THE *ARCHITECTURE A PENSER* **OF PHILIPPE STARCK**

T o evaluate Starck's architectural activity using the traditional standards of criticism is a virtually impossible task.

Starck himself defies every categorisation, and, speaking about his work, has often remarked: '. . . I'm not a designer. I'm not an architect. I'm not a specialist . . . I'm not specialised in anything, which means I'm specialised in everything. As are . . . the majority of people. And I want to get in other people's shoes. I've designed hotels, toothbrushes, lamps, chairs, tables, every kind of object. But the product in itself doesn't mean anything. As far as I'm concerned, it's just an excuse to get involved in something else, in what life could be, for example . . . To sum it all up, I consider myself to be a political agitator who uses design and architecture . . . This is my real occupation.'[1]

The difficulty of criticism increases when confronted with what we can't avoid calling 'the Starck phenomenon', in other words the multiplication of his fame and commitments starting in the mid-eighties, which has made him the subject of scrutiny by the international press. This is an interest which is all too often iconographic and journalistic, and which, with its constant fixation on the character, has hindered the decanting and distancing necessary for an evaluation concerned with more than the image and the most evident and easily grasped aspects.

The fast spread of information on his activities has contributed to the formation of a cult phenomenon amongst the new generations. Followers and emulators are already working *à la* Starck. The mannerism, or rather the soulless vulgarisation that derives from it, has produced a visual contamination which makes it harder to focus on the real bearing of his work.

This, however, is counterbalanced by the almost total silence of the architectural critical establishment which has yet to admit the French 'non-architect' to its own empyrean.

Starck has been working for years within a territory far removed from the *querelle* between Postmodernists and the standard-bearers of the High Tech that today dominates the architectural panorama.

Starck employs different means from the introversion which has pushed a great part of contemporary architecture towards a new sort of nineteenth-century style academic stoicism, or its banally pompous structures. Above all, he is travelling towards a different destination: to use his discipline as an instrument – like a step-ladder which is later abandoned – in order to participate, with the sensibility typical of the end of this century, in the great anthropological transformation that is currently taking place.

Swinging between Utopia and new, end of the millennium sensitivity, Starck is aware of the developments in micro-electronics and genetic engineering, of the interactions between the biological body and the cybernetic body. To be able to read his architecture one doesn't need a dictionary of modern or contemporary architecture, but rather a knowledge of the works of writers like William Burroughs, James G Ballard, Philip K Dick and William Gibson, or familiarity with the films of Ridley Scott, David Cronenberg and Peter Greenaway (*Alien*, *The Fly*, *Videodrome*, *Blade Runner*, *The Belly of an Architect*).

Starck has given himself the task of assuming the double role of protagonist of the new mutations of fantasy, therefore of mankind, and at the same time of critical figure of future destinies.

Disenchantment and passion, awareness of an impending apocalypse and the indelible notion of progress that could lead to the dawn of a new era bind themselves in his work, under the sign of a restlessness which is the spleen of this society at its more advanced heights.

Starck's architecture is at times metaphysical and surreal, at times enigmatic, but always full of tumbles, of role reversals, of the negation of rules and of established, taken for granted relationships. The translation of this restless state, though, doesn't take place in a merely literary/descriptive fashion, but in terms of a strong emotional involvement, and relies on the empathy, the dynamic relationship that can exist between objects and people, and moreover, between people themselves.

His architecture doesn't express itself through the usual terms, such as door/handle, stairs/floor, balcony/roof, floor/covering, but uses a different language: darkness/light, soft/hard, going up/going down, open/shut. These are all terms related to actions or movements that Starck endeavours to make clearer and more evident through a design deviance which forces a conscious awareness of the action that's being performed.

Nothing is taken for granted or as definitive, everything has to be recreated, from objects to behaviours. This way an object remains inanimate until it's possible for it to create a kind of suspense, either by breaking down its function or some other way of resolving it, whereby it assumes new meanings which are also, at times, symbolic. At the same time, the functionalism of architecture is not denied or identified with the ultimate purpose; each of its elements becomes part of a *mise-en-scène*, of an almost film-like quality, that is conducive to a physical and visual adventure which forces an intriguing symbiosis between work and user.

Whilst in the classic concept the voyage is always one of return (to origins, to the home . . .), for Starck this possibility no longer exists.

The only thing worthy of attempt is the run ahead: the lucid, disenchanted, even rough exploration of the territory of what has yet to happen; a kind of obligatory, almost suicidal plunge into the black hole of a future that everything contributes to envisage as disastrous and terrible.

The black streak in Starck and his global pessimism are toned down by a strong dose of irreverence and confidence in a progress that seems able to attack the terrifying monolithic weight of the possible and real negatives that oppress mankind today.

Going to the end of the world, though, to the end of chartered territories, can also mean the discovery of a new world: this is Starck's challenge.

In the accounts that Starck has given us of his development[2], we can glimpse the beginning and growth of this swinging between a strong interest in technological progress and a pessimistic and catastrophic existentialist conception, which has become the cipher to his work.

His father was, amongst other things, an aeronautical engineer: 'My father had matured the idea that research in all fields is almost a duty in life, a kind of obligation. We must invent, it is our place, our mission. Culture, the notion of taste, was subordinate to this research. Just as well to make a creative mistake rather than be holed up in a state of stagnation in good taste. That has partly influenced me; it's part of my heritage, always wanting to create, be creative . . . My father lived all that on a daily basis, he lived for patents, copyrights, whether it was an anti-slip system for ship decks, aeroplane wings, geometric formulae applicable to aeronautics, or helixes for lip-sticks. My father would feel ill if he hadn't had an idea throughout the whole day . . . My father's planes were famous for the better performance they gave . . . always ahead of their time, presenting completely new solutions . . . everybody was talking about the design and the magnificent curves, the sweep of the winged-sections of the Starck planes.'

His often declared disinterest in practices dealing with aesthetics is borne directly from the daily contact with the aerodynamic forms of his father's planes. In a plane everything must concur towards an economy of means, which is also an expressive economy, and no space can be given to gratuity or exuberance. The structural and stylistic repertory of the past is of no use to the form of a plane: new forms must be invented by necessity, there is no umbilical cord with memory and tradition. 'When you look at my pieces of furniture, you'll find, I think, the same tensed curves, the same care for economy, the non-judgement on the form. The form derives . . . essentially from the resolution of its function . . . I really perceive the sensation of the tensing of the lines . . . It becomes more and more noticeable that a tensed curve or the joining of two tensed curves is more interesting than a square.'[3]

The social life goes along the same lines: ' . . . I was unsociable. I tried for a while, then I gave up . . . All the earthly abnormalities were upon me. I was very interested in sensory perception and the environment. I used to work the entire day, for days on end, on the ways of perceiving the house rather than those of living in it, or that sort of thing . . . I used to build prototypes for furniture with gelatines and pastes inside them. I used to drive around the woods on my moped, I was out on my own all day long . . . In those days I used to design mainly underground military bases, of the *Guns of Navarone* variety, very sophisticated chambers of torture, elevators . . . On the whole I can't really say I enjoyed myself. I might as well say it was a permanent state of nightmare, of total neurosis.'

I am essentially morbid; I must not stop thinking about my work, my projects, my little nonsenses, because the minute I have a moment to myself, I have horrible thoughts.

Horrible thoughts on everything. I'm essentially sinister and morbid.

I'm one of the most sinister people available on the market. I have a very peculiar relationship with death; I'm *in* it.

All of our actions are nothing more than struggles to try and exist; so, because I'm always 'a little more' – they call me *Monsieur Plus*, like in the TV ads – I exist a little more. I must always do a little more.[4]

By his own admission, Starck tangentially lives the events of '68 in Paris and his attendance at the École Camondo, and the beginning of his dealings with the Quasar company (where he designed inflatable houses), Pierre Cardin (furniture and chairs in polyurethane and leather), the Italy of industrial design (where he proposed furniture designs and prototypes which, although then refused, were produced in years to come with enormous success), the abortive attempt at self-production between 1979 and 1980 with 'Starck Product', and travelling around the world for two years: ' . . . I've no interest whatsoever in learning about foreign countries, the interest lies within living outside our own codes, our own contexts, living the experience of a cultural deprivation from which one emerges destroyed or an adult. It's not about encountering other designers either. The principal activity lies in observing the rubbish tips, visiting S&M bars, exploring the most secluded aspects of human life.'

I could say I'm a great expert on international politics and economy.

I'm an expert because, and I'm not joking, I look at people's rubbish rather than at their exhibitions. In Tokyo, twenty years ago, the first time I went there, I went up and down the same road for the entire length of my stay.

I did the same in the United States, and I used to open every door that would open; I tried all the doors of every building, every basement, everything; I even entered people's homes . . . And, usually, once I'd been through two or three blocks, I would pick up a rubbish bin and take it back to my hotel room. The contents of a rubbish bin are very interesting; a lot more interesting than what people have to say, or the exhibition at the local museum. They are very much an analysis of the subconscious signs of society: they can't lie. Rubbish bins don't lie.

In 1977 the Società Ubik was founded, the sign for which is still affixed to the door of Starck's Parisian offices (named as a tribute to one of Philip K Dick's most famous novels), and in 1978 'Le Bains-Douches' Night Club, 'hard' and unconventional for a metropolitan people of the night.

In the works of Philip K Dick, Starck has evidently found an affinity with his own sensibilities: from the restless confidence in the human progress – ' . . . It is not brutal instinct that keeps us in a constant state of restlessness and dissatisfaction . . . I'll tell you what it is: it's man's most noble purpose . . . the need to perfect himself . . . of finding new things, of conquering new spaces, of having new experiences. To break from monotony, to go ahead, to progress. To continue to move . . .'[5] – to the unlikelihood of a salvation, rendered impossible by a grandiose and oppressive climate, combined with existential and social themes.

My role is paradoxical: personally, I have nothing to do with anything, I have no respect for anything, I could die any minute; I think that everything is relative, that nothing exists. I think that I only exist because you are looking at me, and that you exist because I'm talking to you. Therefore, nothing really has any importance; so, at the same time, I'm a kind of senseless train, irresponsible and deluded, which is the train of progress; everybody takes the train, or rides an open-top car with a bottle of champagne, and everybody laughs . . . it doesn't bother me, I find it very amusing.

It's all poetry, and really the only interesting thing is acting like a fool; and, at the same time, since I'm honest, sometimes I get off the car and say: 'Hey! Look out! We're here!' Therefore I'm a double agent; I'm in and I'm out. I say: 'Look out, we're here. Gentlemen, if someone doesn't agree, speak up now!' Because this is the road we have embarked on; I emphasise it, I caricaturise the whole lot, I make examples so that they hit even harder, so that people understand before it even happens.

Mine is a role of exposing what will happen. Without judging, I say: 'This is what will happen'.

Personally, it makes me laugh, but perhaps it only makes *me* laugh.

This is my way of doing things; it's not cynicism in any way. It's partly poetry, partly alertness, because, evidently, it's all going to end very badly; everything is going to end horribly badly, in one way or another.

What I'm hoping for now is that we'll get over the archaic phase of the struggle. I'm not convinced though, because not everyone has the degree of evolution that we possess. In the civilised countries, we can now reach what is virtually the final phase of which I've been speaking, of oblivion, of screaming, of slow disintegration.

But some elements now arriving on the scene are 'barbarians', who are not yet prepared for the worst, and who still want to fight; this is so ridiculous!

We don't know what's going to happen.

Philip K Dick, the author of *Do Androids Dream of Electric Sheep* [6] (upon which Ridley Scott based his film *Blade Runner*, which also sums up many other aspects of Dick's work), has developed throughout his production (from *The Man in The High Castle* to *The Simulacra*, from *Dr Bloodmoney*, or *How he Got Along After the Bomb* to *Ubik*) an apocalyptic and hallucinated viewpoint, grotesque and anti-realistic, 'profoundly nourished by elements of mass culture, critical towards its conformist expressions, nonetheless openly contaminated by its own techniques'. [7]

In Dick's universe, in which the places of the standardised and transitory technological world have lost uniqueness and character (Marilyn Monroe, New Jersey is the same as Los Angeles or Tokyo), people read the *Homeopaper* in the morning, the most

TOUS
DIEU
MAIS LES MAITRES
SONT AILLEURS

Philippe Starck,
drawing, undated

appreciated interplanetary currency is the 'truffle skin', mankind travels in 'sealed inter-building commuting vehicles' wearing 'the grey force-field helmet, the short-sleeved shirt, and the red satin shorts popular amongst businessmen', 'the mood organ' programmes awakenings, the androids of Nexus-6 are more 'human' than humans, life and death, like fiction and reality, are confused with each other, and the *Kipple*, a sort of enormous mass of garbage and useless objects, lurks everywhere attacking everything and everybody.

In the great frenzied and grotesque canvas that is Postmodern society, the struggle of Dick's characters is aimed at locating the possibility of some semantic fragment, and reclaiming their own authenticity by attempting to overcome the alienation typical of the modern social organisation. Dick, again: 'To live in such a way that you're always coming across surprises demonstrates that you're not paranoid. There are no surprises for the paranoid; everything happens exactly the way he had foreseen, everything finds a place within his system. It's not possible for us to have a system. Perhaps all systems, in other words all the verbal, symbolic and semantic formulations which pretend to explain the universe with universal hypotheses, are manifestations of paranoia. We must correct ourselves with mysteries, absurdities, contradictions, hostility, but also with the generosity that our environment offers us. It may not be much, but it's always better than the mortal and defeatist certainties of the paranoid.'[8]

The idea of service (of 'comfort') forms the basis of Starck's design activity. All the objects and the architectural designs themselves do not possess autonomous values, but are stimuli, 'fertile surprises' for the fulfilment of better living conditions. To this end they necessarily have to get hold of the collective subconscious (the 'rubbish bin that doesn't lie'), which today is dominated by antisocial and schizophrenic streaks and by a diffused sense of doom and death (divine, ethical, biological, ecological . . .)

My work is about the transformation of 'obligations' into something else; it's an addition of soul.

What I'm saying is that when I'm forced to consume, to expiate this consumption, I inject it with soul, until the object becomes something else, or becomes a small poetic part.

This is typified in my work on the toothbrush.

True, we are obliged to brush our teeth, and we are therefore forced to keep a toothbrush in our bathroom – can't dispute that – but, with a bit of effort we notice that suddenly . . . *voila*! it becomes something else; a flame, a ray of light, an object . . .

In this case I've been successful in my job; I haven't consumed anything, haven't cost society anything, I've simply brought some added value.

The only thing I remember from school is: 'Inanimate objects: Do you have a soul?' I thought it was a good question, in an era when we were surrounded by material objects: Do they have a soul? So I try to give them a soul. I think that because human beings get further and further separated, and become more and more schizophrenic and autonomous, I try to substitute, to give a soul to what surrounds us, to give a little comfort.

The surrealist warning 'on how fragile (human) thoughts are and on what unstable foundations and basements they have erected their insecure homes'[9], is still functional regarding the criticism of a reality invaded by electronic signals and technological simulacra, the dominance of which can bring about collective death and destruction.

In the allegory of *The Man in the High Castle,* in which the forces of the Axis (Death) have won the war against mankind, the feeling of the new Masters' deathly oppression is summarised thus: 'Their view; it is cosmic. Not a man here, a child there, but an abstraction: race, land . . . the abstract is real, the actual is invisible to them . . . It is their sense of space and time. They see through the here, the now, into the vast black deep beyond, the unchanging. And that is fatal to life. Because eventually there will be no life; there were once only the dust particles in space, the hot hydrogen gases, nothing more, and it will come again. This is an interval, *ein Augenblick*. The cosmic process is hurrying on, crushing life back into the granite and methane . . . And these – these madmen – respond to the granite, the dust, the longing of the inanimate; they want to aid *Nature*.'[10]

The Sunset Boulevard of mass society is, in Dick, brightened by the blurred colours of atomic explosions and populated by a disjointed human race forced to coexist with the new monsters.

Dick's black vision of the alarming everyday world is, however, often seen through ironic eyes (the sense of the ridiculous is inseparable from the authentic vision) and relies on the empathy, or in other words, on the capacity typical of the human being to participate emotionally in other people's lives: 'The measure of a man is not his intelligence. It is not how high he rises in the freak establishment. The measure of a man is this: how swiftly can he react to another person's needs? And how much of himself can he give?'[11]

Nature is a lost myth in a totally artificial universe. Realistically, the only thing left is the possibility of a minimalist anthropology made of 'soul supplements', stimuli, 'added values'.

I don't see myself as being particularly inspired by nature, I'm not interested in nature as such; I'm only interested in the confrontation between the human being and nature.

I'm not interested in either animals, vegetables or landscapes; I'm essentially interested in the human being. The cat is very gentle but it doesn't speak, and I don't want to spend my life talking to a dog or a cat when I know that in doing so I renounce being in touch with absolutely thrilling people who have raised human thought to high levels. I've never spent my time sitting on a horse, I don't give a damn.

Dick's nihilism is tempered only by this sense of confidence: 'The world of the future, in my view, is not a place, but an event . . . in which there are only so many characters in search of a plot. Well, there is no plot. There's only them, what they do and what they say to each other, what they build to support each other individually and collectively, like a great parasol that lets the light through, but not the darkness.'[12]

To the characters of *Ubik*, Philip K Dick's novel in which everything is possible thanks to a spray can of the same name, Starck dedicates the first series of furniture, which, from 1982, enjoyed an extraordinary success: the chairs – 'Francesca Spanish', 'Van Vogelsang', 'Wendy Wright', 'Miss Dorn', 'Miss Wirt', 'Miss Beason', 'Pat Conley', 'Tim Hunter'; the bookcases – 'Al Hammond', 'John Ild', 'Mac Gee', 'Herbert Shoenheit' and 'Howard'; the 'Miss Gee' mobile; the tables – 'Ella Runciter', 'Joe Miller', 'Dole

THERE IS NO FUTURE OR PAST WHEN YOU ARRIVE YOU CANNOT KNOW WHAT TIME IT IS.

Philippe Starck,
text, undated

Melipole', 'Tippy Jackson', 'Nina Freede', 'Joe Ship' and 'Titos Apostos'; and the 'Ray Hollis' ashtray.

The tribute to the master of ubiquity, reversal of roles, and apprehension is evident.

Starck's international success coincided with the furnishing of part of the presidential apartments in the Élysée, where he introduced one of his most radical pieces of furniture, the 'Richard III' armchair, calmly bourgeois even in its aluminium or resin versions, but hollow in the back.

I didn't arrive at architecture in any particular way, in the sense that for me architecture is just another thing, a means of expression like any other. I'm not interested in architecture more than I am in design, fishing or water polo.

As far as I'm concerned, it's a way of expressing oneself like any other. There were people who came to me telling me that I could do architecture, and I believed them; after all, it was at their risk and peril. Apparently they were more happy than disappointed; so, if they propose it to me, I'll do it, but without giving it more importance than designing a toothbrush or an ashtray; to me, it's exactly the same thing.

I'm not usually interested in the final product, that is to say I'm not interested in the materialistic final product.

Generally, I don't even look at it, I don't form an opinion of it, if I do it's a bad one, so I'm not interested in that.

All this is but an excuse: I'd go as far as saying that I don't even know why I do this job, it's almost a job by chance; I believe that one is chosen by a job rather than one choosing a job. This is very true in my case, hence I don't deserve any particular 'sacred cow' status.

What I'm trying to say is that I'm not a designer, I'm not a decorator, I'm not an architect: I'm like everyone else, perhaps a little larger, with the same problems, the same dissatisfaction when I look around, with the good luck of having a bad character and of being a little chatty; someone with the ultimate fortune of being given the gift of words, and who consequently uses them not to fight revolutions, but simply to attempt a sequence of small evolutions, putting forward a number of them, frequently, and in various areas at the same time, in many guises. Someone who is simply trying to put forward suggestions for a better lifestyle, aids to living, and hoping, even having the pretence of hoping, that if people live better they'll work harder at it.

My job is essentially didactic, that's why it's pretentious; it's a job that involves propositions which are at the disposal of people. It is for this reason that I work on many things at the same time, because everything is, in fact, an excuse. A building is an excuse, I use it for its dimension, for its nature, to make something of it in some sense or another; a toothbrush is another excuse, all this has no importance.

By using the pretext of the architecture of interiors (La Main Bleue (1976), 'Les Bains-Douches' (1978), Le Chalet du Lac, the Centre Ville), Starck approaches the architectural sector by way of refining a method of semantic *mise-en-scène,* which on the one hand describes the intimate history of the genesis of the project, and on the other is capable of involving with hypnotic power, and which will find its first completed form in Café Costes (1984).

Here the *mise-en-scène* of super-dimensions (the circular pillars, the staircase), of colour values which are certainly not strong or exuberant, (pale greens, greys, browns) and of unnerving details (the clock with the wrong hours, the false skylight), confers an alienating effect to the place, an effect of a suspended dimension beyond the usual codes. The invitation to undertake the metaphorical voyage into another dimension is enhanced by the ostentatious central staircase.

The staircase is very important to me, because I never do anything gratuitous. I never spend a franc or a gram of energy doing something that could be defined as stylistic or decorative. I do nothing else but satisfy requirements; I'm required to go from one level to the next, therefore I need to have a staircase. Then, I take this staircase and . . . almost make it the central element, because it's an element I'm interested in, because the staircase is, typically, symbolically and functionally a scene, a theatrical scene. It's always been like that, in magazines . . . everywhere. You go up a staircase, you descend a staircase . . . it's a scene by definition, and I'm interested in dealing with theatrical scenes to place people in another reality and make them live another moment in time. I make staircases which are theatre scenes, where people are given value, where, for a brief moment, people can be stars, as Warhol used to say.

This is what I'm interested in.

I never gratuitously decide to install a scene; rather, I'm told a staircase is needed, and the staircase becomes a scene. Everything, everything, everything . . . I have no imagination, no dreams, no desires.

I'm simply told that toilets are needed, and I'll make magnificent toilets; I'm told to go from one level to the next, and I'll make the most incredible staircase; I'm told, I don't know . . . a cash register is needed, and I'll make a symbolic, semantic till, that signifies something. At the same time, if in the washroom they need a hand dryer, it will become something else.

The staircase, with its semantic values of physical passage (from one place to the next) and of mental passage (from one condition to another, from earth to sky, from perdition to salvation) is a characteristic element of Starck's other works (Maison Lemoult, the Manin Restaurant, Starck's first house, 'Moon Dog' . . .).

The same significance is assumed by the chequerboard in Starck's linguistic repertory: symbol of ubiquity, of the human condition as a pawn in an unintelligible and irrational game.

In *The Square of the Cities* (1965) by John Brunner, the Utopian city of the future is the scene of a collective madness, where 'anybody . . . from the President down to the girl with the guitar, were puppets dancing at the mercy of forces uncontrollable by the single individuals.'

In 'The World of Starck' the chequerboard is the symbol for an unnerving, all-encompassing levelling-out that has already taken place, where definitions of places have been lost, and where human beings wander aimlessly. In the Parisian branch of Mercedes-Benz, the symbolic flooring is chequered (the base, the ground, the human condition); as are the planned exteriors of the Maison Lemoult, and Starck's first house, 'Moon Dog'; the space outside the Laguiole factory; the riverside area in the 'Rue Starck'; and 'Toar'.

'Feet in the mud and head in the stars' is one of Starck's mottoes derived from 'Cyberpunk' literature: from the chequerboard to the stars through a journey (the staircase) which must be both modern and alive. 'Matter is slow and the spirit fast. The

Philippe Starck, Maison Lemoult,
preliminary sketch, 1987

23

Philippe Starck, Maison Lemoult,
preliminary sketch, 1987

dream moves at the speed of light, the body at that of the feet. To be modern today one needs to have the head in the stars and feet in the mud. A good balance; difficult, but good.'[13]

In accordance with his philosophy of 'non-professionalism' and non-integration, Starck, like a 'hacker' or a 'rocker', prefers to be the hybrid inhabitant of an inter-zone surrounded by a small 'tribe of non-idiots', his friends and collaborators of many years.

Starck's own working methods are evidently anomalous compared to the traditional ways of operating a professional studio, but it is clear in its intents: to provide ideas, know-how, grey matter: the supports for life, apocalyptic but not integrated.

Architecture is very similar to what I generally do, except for the final stage; which is to say that I absorb pieces of information, always by myself, I compare them . . . it is essentially the work of my subconscious; I never work consciously, I'm incapable of it.

I'm not someone who can be defined as intelligent, in other words someone possessing reasoning structures. I'm someone who has needs for reasoning, but not reasoning structures.

That's it, I essentially work through reasoned intuitions.

Therefore, my greatest work is a work of concentration and de-concentration; in other words I absorb the data, I slowly think about it (you could even say I don't think about it, that's closer to the truth) and at a certain time I'm alerted, I'd say by my 'biology' rather than my brain, that my project is ready.

I then know it's ready but I don't know what it is. At this point, always by myself, I take a pencil and piece of paper, as usual, and I draw the project: fifteen minutes for the first idea, one hour to finalise it, and three hours (one afternoon) to go into details and finalise absolutely everything. In general, after three hours and three sheets of A4, everything's done, it's all there: interiors, exteriors, sometimes the furnishings, the communication of the product, the name, even the different ideas around it. Then, you could say, I'm no longer involved in it.

After that, my team takes over and makes nice drawings simply by using my sketches enlarged in the photocopier . . . My team then goes into the reality of things, that is to say they really design the detail of the hinges, etc . . . It's a team that's very close to me, which has been working with me for ten years. It's a very small tribe . . . there are only two people.

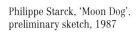

Philippe Starck, 'Moon Dog',
preliminary sketch, 1987

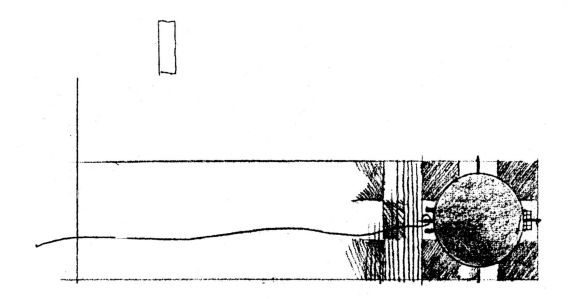

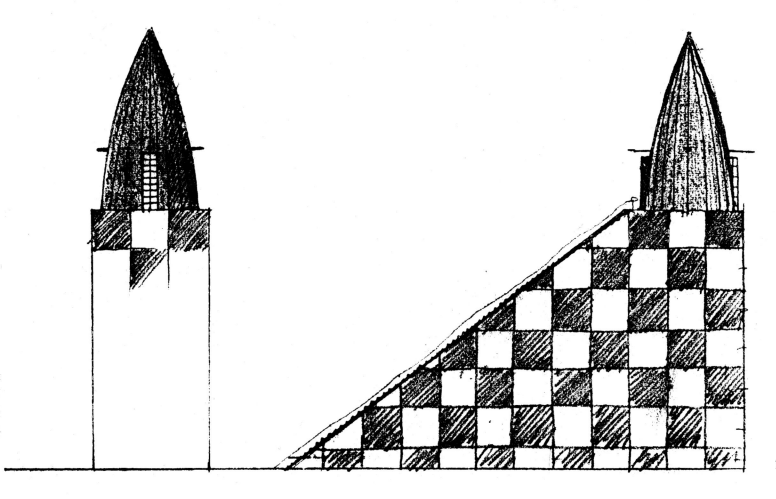

Philippe Starck,
text, undated

DES LIEUX ET DES GENS DE LIEUX

CALDER POUR AVOIR FAIT DE L'ART AVEC UN BOUT DE FIL DE FER

ACHILLE CASTIGLIONI POUR AVOIR INVENTER DU QUOTIDIEN AVEC UN BOUT DE FICELLE

GAUDI POUR AVOIR EU L'INTUITION ORGANIQUE

MENDELSON POUR LUI AVOIR DONNE UNE SUITE MODERNE

DAVID LYNCH POUR AVOIR MIS L'AIR EN VIBRATION

WIM WENDERS POUR NOUS AVOIR FAIT AIMER LES IMAGES MEME D'AMERIQUE

PIERRE CHAREAU POUR AVOIR INVENTE LA MAISON INTELLIGENTE

LA MER DE GLACE POUR ETRE SOUS LA GLACE

DENIS SANTA CHIARA POUR ETRE UN INVENTEUR ET NON UN STYLISTE

ALBERTO MEDA POUR ~~POUR~~ AVOIR APPORTE L'ELEGANCE DE L'INGENIERIE

FRANK GEHRY POUR ETRE LIBRE DANS UN PAYS QUI NE L'EST PAS

TADAO ANDO POUR ETRE MYSTIQUE DANS UN PAYS QUI NE L'EST PLUS

FRANCESCO CLEMENTE POUR ETRE TELLEMENT LUI MEME

SHIRO KURAMATA POUR AVOIR PARLE DE L'INVISIBLE

ALESSANDRO MENDINI POUR REFLECHIR POUR NOUS

AFRA , CARLO , TOBIA SCARPA POUR AVOIR PROUVE QUE DIEU EST DANS LE DETAIL

CHARLES EAMES POUR ETRE UN AMERICAIN ELEGANT

JEAN LUC GODARD POUR NOUS AVOIR REAPPRIS A ECOUTER

JENNY HOLZER POUR NOUS PROTEGER " FROM WHAT I WANT "

LA RUE PIERRE DE NOLHAC A VERSAILLES POUR NOUS RAPPELER QUE LA VILLE

DOIT ETRE UNE SCENE

JAMES TURREL POUR NOUS AVOIR MONTRE LE CIEL

LA CASA MALAPARTE , QUE TOUTES LUI RESSEMBLENT

LOU REED POUR AVOIR CREE UN UNIVERS MUSICAL

It's a very friendly, very informal relationship; we only do the minimum necessary. There are two kind of people: those who search and those who find; we have the fortune of being part of the latter. By this I mean that when we take a design to someone, whoever they may be, we bring only one sheet, or the maquette: we put it down, and, generally, it's all right. Usually, project presentations are terrible – they go on for two or three minutes, and then you don't know what to say. We elaborate, we discuss designs that we liked, or that are important . . . [Anything else] seems useless to us, when everything can be resolved in a couple of minutes, because we work on the evidence of things.

So, unlike those who bring hundreds of sheets and notes with them to explain how they reached the solution, when we haven't found a solution (and it happens once or twice a year), we say: 'We haven't found it. We haven't found a solution, give us another week or two.' But when we arrive, it's really with the bare essentials; we are not paper or maquette salesmen. When the work of the team is finished (and it is conceptual work, never of realisation), only then do we pass it on to a good studio which will take care of the actual realisation.

We completely separate the conception of a design from its execution; it's not the same job, it shouldn't even have the same name.

The vital urgency of the job doesn't even allow for stopping to consider history. In the work of reconstructing the universe (whether it is almost futuristic, as with Depero, or in a more up-to-date style, as with Raymond Loewy), there is no possibility of looking at a past which is unable to give an answer to the pressing questions posed by the innovations of technology and the new post-industrial landscape.

There is only time for a few declarations of love, and for admitting that the past does indeed exist, and is lived . . .

'Unconsciously' – I don't remember anything, mine is a profoundly amnesiac process. I'm a pathological amnesiac, seriously. Just to give you an example, a while ago I didn't know where I had parked my car, I couldn't remember. I'm incapable of remembering what I did yesterday, totally incapable.

I had to pay a parking fee for twenty-four hours because I couldn't remember at what time I had arrived.

I can't say that I have any influences (from the past) that I can honestly recognise. There are people who I love, that is to say, who I admire: Gaudi and Mendelsohn. So there are people who I love dearly . . . but that's it. One can certainly find influences in Mendelsohn, the Einstein Observatory, for example; after that I wouldn't know . . .

The way I work is a 'magma', in other words a pile, a shapeless grouping of unprocessed pieces of information, augmented by a multitude of micro-informations. It's similar to the way whales live; I have the body and feeding method of a whale. That is to say that the whale absorbs, it never eats large fish. It absorbs tonnes of krill, of plankton, every day. And so I live totally by the wayside. I don't go to the cinema, to exhibitions, to the theatre, I don't watch TV, and when people talk to me I don't understand them . . . On the other hand everybody knows that, so nobody talks to me, it's more practical.

I only talk nonsense, I only hear nonsense, so all the better for it.

I'm weary of the great ideas, of the good and nice ideas, because they are the first ones to be perverted, they are the first to backfire (we can all see what happened to Christianity and Communism); these are all basically good ideas which then ended up biting their tails at some point.

Consequently, out of laziness, out of deep schizophrenia, and out of indifference, I much prefer to look at the colour of a sock, a light, the fragment of what I'm told about a film and its distortion. It is first distorted by the those telling me about it, then by me because I don't understand them . . . Many formless things like that ensure that I'm rarely mistaken. It's like the way a computer works; a computer has no great movements, just millions of yes, no, yes, yes, no, yes, no, no, yes'. It's the same for me: I'm like a magma of yes' and nos, but the results are reasonably good (even though there is no choice).

Three works of 1985 make reference to the high technology and 'tensed curves' of Starck's father's planes: the multipurpose hall in the Musée des Arts Décoratifs, the Cartier Bridge, and the design for the 'Art et Industrie' exhibition, in which functions are hidden behind circumspect forms: the wing of the *Super Constellation* adored by the native tribe.

From the outset of his architectural activity, Starck has forced the blatant asceticism and the pretentious rationality of High Tech culture to a dilemma, exposing them as new myths and even worse, as elements vital to a universe devoid of significance. If the

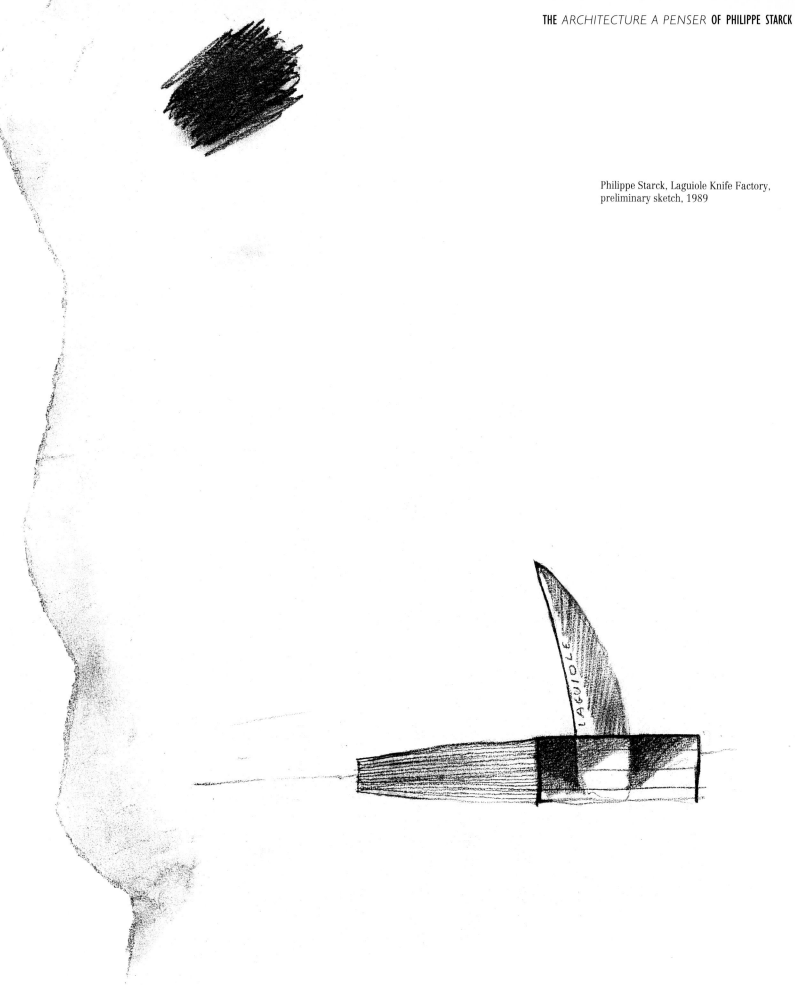

Philippe Starck, Laguiole Knife Factory,
preliminary sketch, 1989

most radical nonsense is death, the purpose of life, and perhaps even its vanity, consists of the search for meanings. Architecture cannot elude its semantic mission.

Therefore, in terms of movements, with all of today's great currents (Postmodernism, Neoclassicism, 'Technicism', 'Transparency'), it is possible that some of them could emerge to be the final standard; you might say that what I call 'Technicism' and 'Transparency' could be the ultimate standards.

I don't believe it. I don't criticise anything, except for Neoclassicism and the degeneration of Postmodernism.

I criticise the basis of Neoclassicism, right from its origins; I criticise not the starting point of Postmodernism, but rather what it has turned into. Apart from that, I find myself completely in agreement with 'Technicism' and I'm perfectly in accordance with 'Transparency'. On the whole, though, I'm in agreement with everything; I find there's room for everything.

I simply believe that some of these great standards, which might appear to be the great final standards, are inevitably not so: I also believe that amongst all this there's a little place for another way, which is what I might call 'Expressionist Architecture'.

It could be the right term – even though I refer to it in two ways: in industrial design I call it 'Emotive Style', and in architecture 'Expressionist Architecture' (though I don't know why I make the distinction, because they can easily cross over).

I have no worthwhile judgement on architecture in cultural terms, nor in terms of beauty, or aesthetics . . . I haven't got the faintest idea, I'm not interested.

The relationship of light and shade, of volumes, of proportions . . . leaves me completely cold. As far as public buildings are concerned, I deal with either semantics (pure semantics) or giving emotions. The purpose of these emotions is to scrutinise people, to wake them up, to transform them from becoming more and more passive spectators into actors.

My role is principally that of an agitator. That is to say that there are two roles, the more serious which is didactic, and the other which is that of agitator, albeit without the taste for provocation or aggression, but one which simply seeks to ask people: see if this building can be something else, if a toothbrush could be this, if a bicycle could be that . . . maybe you could be something else, or your life could be something else.

So wake up, work on your lifestyles, work on your cities, on your society, on your civilisation. This is what I'm trying to say, mainly, and I'll say it again: I work with the means that they give me.

All this applies principally to public architecture, which goes from the outside inwards. Private architecture – of which I don't do much and that for me isn't the same job (it shouldn't even bear the same name) – is of a completely different nature; it goes from the inside outwards . . . here I'm not interested in art, culture or semantics, here I'm only interested in the small qualities of life, the small pleasures, the private thing, the happy moment . . . the nice kitchen that lights up when you have breakfast, the proximity of the bathroom, the log fire: essentially, the small-scale comforts. In other words, in this place there is total humility.

I find that I arrive at the front elevations quite naturally, without working. It is nothing other than the comfort of people that expresses itself on the facades of their homes, with fresh, almost new, and quite timeless results, for the good reason that they're hardly designed at all; whatever is due to happen, happens; the window is there where it should be . . .

The people who come to me are people whom I love (I like them, they like me); we are a little alike, we think the same way; and since we both have two eyes, a nose and two legs . . . I design as if it were for myself, and, apparently, it works very well.

What I'm saying is that I'm honest enough to put myself in the position of saying: I'm not here to make fun, I'm not here to be a clown, to take advantage of it; I ought to be able to live here: therefore it is a work of total honesty.

So for me it's two different jobs. In this case it's not a semantic excuse, it really is work based on the quality of people's lives; not in a metaphorical way as with public buildings, which are essentially buildings of image.

The double standard indicated by Starck isn't always applied. Function, decor and symbols cross over quite clearly even in projects which are not the most eminent or representative examples of his architectural work.

In the Manin restaurant, the staircases have evidently assumed the semantic role of the union and separation of an alien space; almost the reconstruction of an earthly environment in the extra-world, with reality. In Starck's first home, in Montfort-L'Amaury,

Philippe Starck, 'Nani Nani',
preliminary sketch, 1989

again we find the chequerboard, the staircase for a symbolic ascension to the heavens, the mannequin pillars inspired by Giorgio de Chirico. Starck even dedicates the flooring of the Teatriz Restaurant to the master of 'philosophical painting', in an explicit admission of affinity to the discovery of 'the demon in all things' (De Chirico) and to the realisation that enigmas and the unsettling lurk around every street corner. For the painter of the metaphysical 'New World' in which fiction and reality, memory and vision, conscious and subconscious blend in with each other, the central myth is always Odysseus (the return voyage searching for the self), whilst for a Postmodern conscience the recuperation in reverse of a paradise lost is no longer possible.

Some of the themes are still useful though, those of unveiling (the curtain in the 'Teatriz' restaurant and its bar downstairs); of the unsettling image (the Sphinx of Maison Lemoult, the ticket booth simulacrum of 'La Cigale', the gigantic knife of Laguiole, the flame of Asahi); of the reversals of roles (the wall padding of the Manin Restaurant, the banister that disappears and reappears on the staircase of the Coppola salon, the many staircases of the Maison Lemoult, the door handles in the windows of Hugo Boss); of the realisation of subconscious obsessions (the enormous truncated black animal of the Tokyo Opera House, the vertiginous abyss inside 'Moon Dog', the zoomorphic monster of 'Nani Nani').

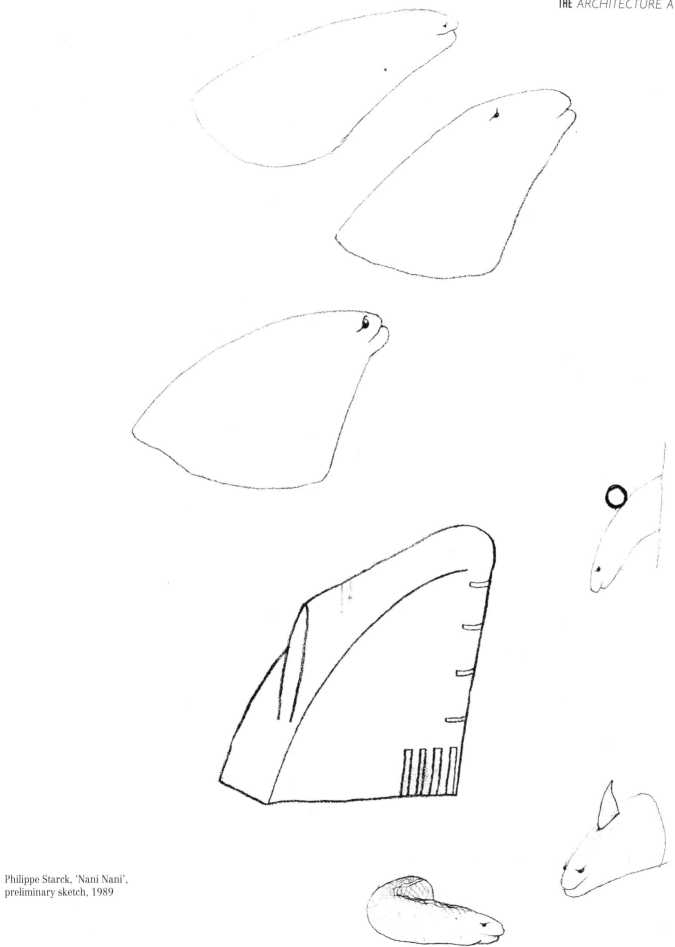

Philippe Starck, 'Nani Nani',
preliminary sketch, 1989

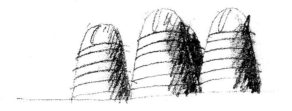

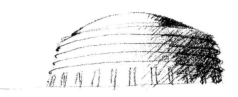

Philippe Starck, Toar,
preliminary sketch, 1992

The strength of Starck's imaginary vision, though, doesn't derive only from his literary premises or his sensitivity to the more advanced social mutations currently taking place. Rather it is found in his medium-like capacity to render physical the new symbols and the new monsters together with the ironic streak that is his trademark.

Starck, as has often been said, does not have a method, does not believe in the linearity and the 'transmittability' of knowledge, and the diversity of his architectural production is the clearest testimony of that. Zoomorphism prevails in Tokyo's Opera House and in 'Nani Nani', a crude stereometry in 'Moon Dog', in the design for the Ecole des Beaux Arts, in Starck's second home, and in 'The Angle', a thrusting comic strip quality in 'Toar', and sophisticated geometrical distortions in the pavilion for the Venice Biennale.

The common denominator is intentional disregard for the norm, and an original surprise effect.

Like a master of cinema, Starck organises set pieces and involving situations. Not by chance one of Starck's most used self-promotion photographs pictures him with his eye set in a small frame, like the magnifying lens in one of Hitchcock's most famous portraits.

Like a cinematic progression, Starck denotes the place and the action with a few immediate strokes, and then sets off a succession of wide angle frames, of sweeping shots, fade-ins, montages and close-ups. The progression of spaces in Teatriz (the great room with the black drape, the up-down slope towards the bar on stage, the slope to the rooms below, the surprises in the washrooms . . .), and in the Royalton and Paramount hotels (sweep shot on the hall, long shot on the staircase, the surprise in the details in the corridors . . .) are already involving screenplays, waiting to be performed. No element is gratuitous or the fruit of unmotivated fantasy, everything contributes to give back significance to the object and the most banal gesture.

Although making reference to themes and symbols of society, Starck remains distanced from the optimistic pretences of the comic-strip-like wave of Memphis and the pessimism of punk counter-culture fostered by the ideology of the global market of trash

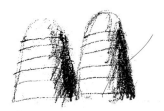

Philippe Starck, Toar,
preliminary sketch, 1992

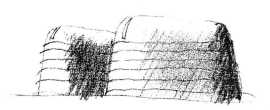

(the 'kipple' of Dick). Symbols and cult objects of this last theme have been the film *Blade Runner* (1982), and William Gibson's successful novel *Neuromancer* (1984).

Symptomatic of this new sensibility is the first description of an interior in *Neuromancer*: 'Neo-Aztec bookcases gathered dust against one wall of the room . . . A pair of bulbous disney-style table lamps perched awkwardly on a Kandinski-look coffee table in scarlet-lacquered steel. A Dali clock hung on the wall between the bookcases, its distorted face sagging to the bare concrete floor. Its hands were holograms that altered to match the convolutions of the face as they rotated, but it never told the correct time.'[14]

Starck, on the other hand – and here is his unmistakable trait – is never descriptive, he never cites, never makes references to the past, to *déjà-vu*, even if reinforced by a dissonant poetry. For Starck, function must translate itself not into image but into action, into event: from the 'Titos Apostos', 'Mickville', 'Dole Melipole', 'Nina Freed' folding tables to the 'Francesca Spanish', 'Mrs Frick', 'Lola Mundo' folding chairs, the bionic bottle for Vittel, the 'Walter Wayle' faceless clock, and the 'Ara' lamp, with its unusual switching system. And for the event to unfold completely a scenography and script which can give an aura of specialness to even the most humble actions and objects is required.

The only elements making up Starck's 'rules' appear to be those of contradiction and transgression. Thus the staircases of the Maison Lemoult lead to too many and improbable accesses; the staircases of the Costes and the Paramount don't follow a straight line; the structures of the Ecole des Beaux Arts are obscured by a sort of glass parallelepiped that envelopes them; padding and tiling cover even ceilings (Manin, Teatriz); buildings acquire astounding weight (Tokyo's Opera); or the appearance of a magnified object (Le Baron Vert); the Coca-Cola logo becomes graffiti (Cafe Mystique); pillars loose their structural value to acquire a bio-morphic quality (Teatriz, Asahi); perpendicularity is forsaken in favour of disarrangements and inclinations (the pavilion at the Venice Biennale, 'The Angle', 'Nani Nani'); awkward elements such as corners or edges are emphasised; and the structural and tectonic elements, the language of architecture, are inessential in the visual rendition of the building ('Nani Nani', Le Baron Vert).

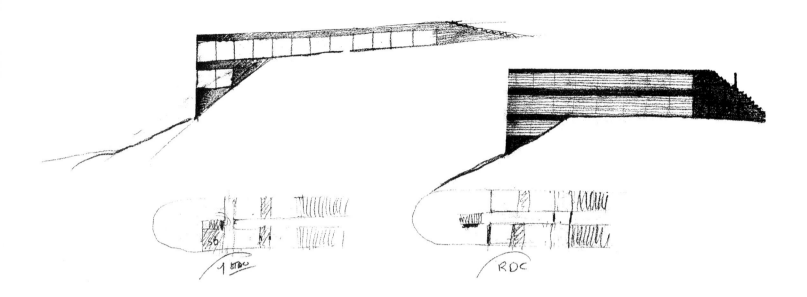

Philippe Starck, Maison Vidalenc,
preliminary sketches, 1992

In Starck's architecture and interiors the irregular trapezium is always preferred to the square or the rectangle. It is exactly these space cut-outs, or rather these additions of space (the small triangles that when added to a rectangle form a trapezium), these 'shadow areas' beyond the obvious, the banal and controllable, that allow for expressiveness and emotion. This also applies on an urban scale.

The theme of proposals for urban development is very clear: it is part of a global plan which states that the town must not be considered in terms of materialism, or architecture, but must be considered as a support for life; in other words, grounds for 'being happy in it', for human development. The rest is of no interest, the great elements, the nice perspectives, the nice landscapes . . . I don't share these ideas, except for my direct willingness to help human beings to be happy, to participate in their lives and their civilisation.

So, if tomorrow I were to be nominated chief town architect (you never know), what I would try to do, would be to give great freedom. I don't think it's possible to have the best, we are forced to have the best as well as the worst; but I think that because life is 'self-cleansing', cities are self-cleansing. That is to say that only the interesting things and the monsters remain; mediocrity disappears little by little, you don't even notice it disappearing.

What I find interesting is a town like a chequerboard, where I'm a little mouse, and where every time I find a chess piece, a queen, a rook, it becomes an emotional event. I want every street corner to be as emotional as people when they watch television. Television today is certainly the strongest conveyor of emotions and non-emotions; today, because society is schizophrenic, people stay home to watch TV, to play Nintendo, and will soon be immersed in virtual reality machines.

Not that we can criticise them today. Why, for what reason should they go out into the streets? What do streets have to offer today? For what reason should they travel? What curiosity would they have to travel to another town? They are all the same, they all have the same equipment. Buildings are all equipped, all I see is equipment; in other words relatively well-made constructions, that shelter people from the rain, the cold, the heat, that sort of thing. But can you make a town out of equipment? Can you wear a necklace made of screwdrivers and hammers? I don't think so.

I think that we must give ourselves the means to make people interested in their towns again, without any kind of vulgarities, venality, nonsense. Therefore I'm about to engage in combat with this

Philippe Starck, text, 1990

ADIEU

IL NOUS FAUT DISPARAITRE

LA BOULE EST VIDE

LA CREATION DEVRA OUBLIER LA MATIERE MAIS PAS LE BUT

IL FAUT SAUTER UNE ETAPE

ON VOULAIT DU CHAUD PAS DES RADIATEURS

ON VOULAIT DE L'EAU PAS DES ROBINETS

L'INERTE DOIT MOURIR

L'ENERGIE DOIT VIVRE

UN SEUL MOT: DISPARITION

cathodic death that spies on us (unless I calm myself later).

I was talking about slogans, emotions at every street corner. What I want to say is that a totally phantasmagorical and very liberated town is being outlined, one which would become increasingly free because I would make sure that there would always be a garden and a courtyard side, always a sunny side and a shady side. In other words there will always be interstices, ungoverned places, cracks, backs, sides, alleyways, areas which escape control, where emotions and humour can really be expressed.

I don't think that great decisions are taken in great conference rooms, I believe that decisions are taken in the corridors of conference rooms.

I will always make sure that there will be these emotions and shadowy areas.

Starck's idea of a town, a sort of global village of telecommunications, puts forward on an almost cosmic level the apprehensions (concerning progress and impotence) in his architecture.

The degree of sophistication attained by technology in the last decade has certainly left its specific disciplinary confines, and has involved, through the mass media and certain kinds of literature (not least science fiction) aspects of communication, art, philosophy and day to day life. The first contributions in this sense can be seen in the exhibition 'Les Immateriaux', held in Paris in 1985, organised by JF Lyotard and T Chaput, and in the book *Dematerialisation and Postmodernism*, also published in 1985 and edited by Lyotard.

The concept of dematerialisation, of the progressive reduction and disappearance of the objects and material elements that surround us in favour of their resolution into pure fluxes of energy, is a possibility offered and promised by technology (a magical luminous ray on which images appear in place of television, the cold in place of the refrigerator, measurable light in place of illumination appliances, the substitution of the traditional wall with windows and curtains with a thermo-regulated and self-obscuring element . . .).

If today it isn't possible to foresee a future arising from this kind of development, all this certainly represents a tendency that Starck considers plausible.

Philippe Starck,
French Pavilion at the
Venice Biennale,
preliminary sketches,
1990

The hypothesis of a new century dotted with intangible realities, images and situations in which it will be difficult, if not impossible, to distinguish reality from illusion is reinforced by the same conditions of today and the ideas that are already thought as possible: the unbelievable can become believable.

Today it is already difficult to make a distinction, in the manifestations of mass society, between things and their simulacra, between illusion and reality, between fiction and truth.

In this tendency Starck is able to glimpse the positive possibility of an acceleration of the spirituality of human life taking place. In any case, as ever, he reserves for himself the double task of indicating the possible, and perhaps inevitable developments of society, and at the same time of pointing out their negative sides.

Perhaps it is because of this that, whilst awaiting a general dematerialisation, Starck proceeds in his task of charging objects (still necessary until radical technological developments) with those affectionate, emotional values of friendly presence and of comfort, which will nonetheless have to be part, perhaps in another form, of the life of the future.

Matter, object, energy are not a contradiction, they are a transition which has been my purpose for some time and through all my production.

I've realised that the 21st century and the ones to follow will necessarily be immaterial. It's the only possible end, the only possible purpose. I think there are a number of parameters by which to reach this conclusion. I think the only real dream of mankind is progress; the idea of progress is simply poetry. Only poetry; nothing explains the need for progress, nothing. I think the only explanation for wanting to progress is the wish to become God, in other words, the wish to believe in what we are told, which is that we have to be the image of God.

Let's ask ourselves: who is God? (I don't believe he exists, I'm strictly atheist, a militant atheist, but I like the idea; it makes me laugh, especially because it works, we have to admit that).

God is someone who is omnipotent and has no flesh, does not have a body and can do anything. I think the only dream of mankind is to be omnipotent and have no flesh; if we analyse the production of mankind from the beginning up to now, all the evidence points to this. All production points to this; if we look at the most recent products, those closer to us, we notice that everything is nothing but an excuse to be like God. The car, an artificial leg to go faster, like God who moves fast; lenses to see further, Like God who sees everything; the calculator, to allow us to think faster, like God who has an enormous capacity to absorb information, because he considers everybody individually; communications, God is everywhere and communicates with everybody at the same time.

The materialism of religion is a funny joke that makes things palpable, so that those with little imagination can believe in something by touching it.

The only thing that excuses religion is this need for something else, this need for unreality. This is one of the first parameters, which brings everything, all the work of mankind, to point towards progress, towards power and miniaturisation, towards what we could call the loss of flesh and body.

A second point is that we have only just understood what Galileo was saying, because until a few years ago we had an Egyptian vision of our planet; in other words, it was a flat vision, a flat and infinite Earth. This was exemplified by our attitude to materials and energy, since we were excavating them as if they were, indeed, interminable. A typically flat vision, only a flat vision can give this idea of infinity.

So we've only recently understood what Galileo was saying, that the Earth is a sphere; a sphere implies the idea of a finite world. We've just understood that the Earth is a closed world which we can't excavate and degrade forever.

Consequently this inevitably brings us to the idea of economy, because the minute that you realise it's a finite world, you must start to think before you cause any damage, produce, excavate or expend energy.

I think we really are at the end of a love story; in other words, matter is tired, the Earth is tired, and we are also tired of matter. After digging for so long, so much that we're surrounded by objects as emotive substrata, I think we're also tired of matter.

Matter is tired, and we are tired of matter. It's the end of a love affair. That is to say that the immediate future will totally reform the conception of producers' working practices: and I am a producer. Which means that the first question is: 'Is it necessary?'

In other words, I think that today I'm in the relatively comfortable position of not being forced into a state of 'urgency'.

Philippe Starck,
drawing, undated

My luxury today is to try to do my job as honestly as possible.

My job, then, is to analyse what my job actually entails. My job is by no means merely that of a producer; my job is that of provider of services. I'm here at the service of society, to help people around me to live better.

It's a crystal clear task!

I think that there was a way of thinking that usually produced the answer through materialism, and that that has caused our position as producers to degenerate; which is to say that if someone wanted cold, instead of reflecting on the 'how' of 'cold', we immediately designed a refrigerator. If someone wanted water, we immediately designed a tap. If someone wanted hot, we immediately designed a heater. The thing is, the heater, the tap, the refrigerator are all globally archaic apparatus, with sweaty feet and smelly armpits, they wear out, they break down; they cost too much, they mainly profit those who produce them and those who sell them. The question today, if you want to do your job honestly, is: 'You want water? Yes, wait, I'll see what I can do.' Maybe it's a problem of chemistry, maybe it's meteorology. 'You want cold? Yes, all right, let me work at this.' Here too it's a problem of, I don't know, biology, physics . . .

Today, though, I place myself in an open position by saying I'm here to provide some services, I'm not here to be a producer who puts talent into it because I have a talent for these things, to produce . . . to rob people: I'm not here to suck blood out of people: their money is their blood, their sweat is their blood.

This is the most radical vision of my position. To really try and do one's job, one's duty.

What is annoying is that the more talent I have, the more it works! Let's not kid ourselves: what am I today? I am a maker of Christmas gifts, that's all. So, because I'm so good, my Christmas presents are better than others, and so museums buy mine more than others. I'll try and do better, and improve this state of things.

This is why the future brings us to immateriality, brings me directly to immateriality.

Because this is so radical, we can't arrive at it in a tick, we must have the means . . . There are provisional settings that have a tendency towards this, but are not yet radical. What I'm saying is that there are moments when we are forced to be materialistic, therefore these settings will apply; there's the setting of the soul, of the soul supplement; there's the setting, provisional, of visibility and magic.

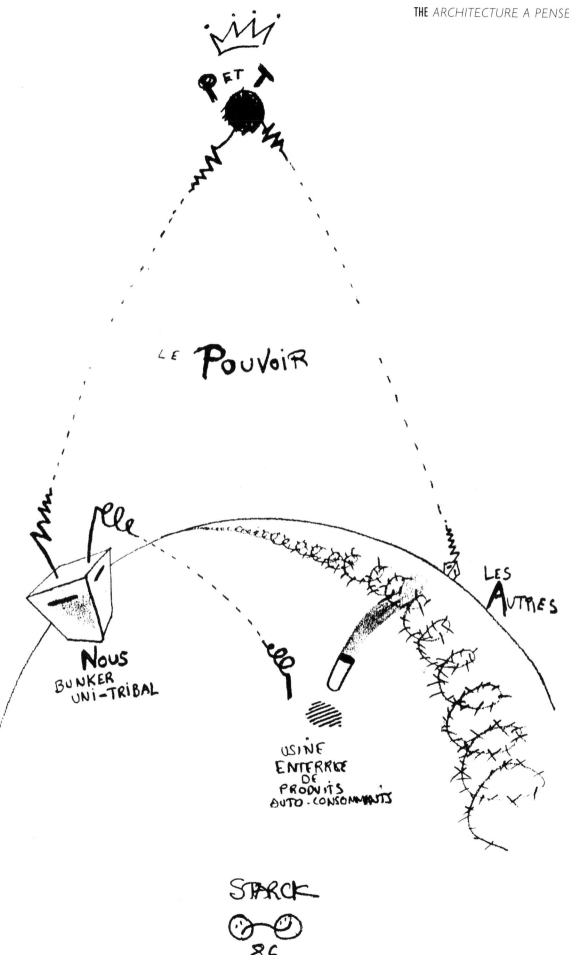

Philippe Starck,
drawing, 1986

Philippe Starck,
drawing, undated

In accordance with his vision of a future dominated by telecommunication, Starck takes to the extreme the concept of dematerialisation until he foresees the disappearance of today's urban, metropolitan, territorial and infrastructural settings.

The architecture of human work will be interred as it is in the post-bomb world in Dick's novel *Autofac*, in which the underground production centres are self-regulated, self-designed and self-reproducing. Communications will take place exclusively via satellite and the home, also a place of work, since the great communication possibilities will render obsolete the necessity of physical movement. The architecture of work will take the form of a coagulation of 'tribes by affinity'.

On the chequerboard of the global village the antiquated characteristics of the environment and of relations will be nullified, and on it will rise buildings which are almost temporary and introverted, because all functions will take place within their interiors and from interior to interior, through images or virtual reality. Roads, squares and territory will no longer be necessary elements.

At the same time, Starck assigns to the exterior of buildings, to their 'chassis' (intended as an appropriate component to cover and envelop the complex internal functions), semantic and strongly communicative values.

To the arresting hypothesis of a world governed by telecommunications and new powers Starck opposes, right from the start, the possibilities of autonomous areas, not managed, not controlled and not controllable.

If, in the near future, the interiors will be the seats of power and control, as in Orwell's *1984*, Starck gives the exteriors and the interstices between them antithetical and strongly expressive values, and 'soul supplements', because only within them can actions and life take place.

It is architecture's destiny to become dated.

It is complicated. First of all, I think there are different kinds of architecture: there's the architecture of utensils, or better still, the architecture of relaxation and the architecture of work. I think that the architecture of work is being buried, in other words, that the architecture of the machines is increasingly

Philippe Starck,
drawing, undated

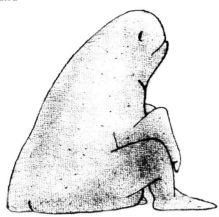

being buried (everything is becoming more and more mechanised, there are fewer and fewer workers in factories, there's no more reason to have windows, no more reason to have air, no more cause for the building to get dirty).

The architecture of human work will be in the place for rest, meaning that people will work in their own homes, through information technology. I have little faith in urban architecture: I believe there will be a proliferation of small forts, of regularly placed citadels that will provide dwellings for tribes with sympathetic affinities – I was saying cultural earlier on – in the lateral sense of sympathetic; in other words, the relations between people: I love you, I don't love you.

I don't think the forts will be trenched, but I think they will lose the means of communicating with each other. I believe there will be a dispersal of forts, a disappearance of roads, trenched factories and deliquescent cities, that will gather the rejects, the outcasts of society.

. . . I believe that everything in the future will be filtered through satellites. I think the biggest problem in the future will be the domination of satellites, which as I've said will mean that people will become more and more isolated; so, instead of talking directly to each other, they'll communicate by reflection. All it will take is for the owners of the satellites to disagree with you, or for you to be of the wrong colour, the wrong party, or the wrong sexual majority, and you'll get 'cut off'. And it's a society that tomorrow will not fight, but forget people.

There will be forgotten people there nearby. People will be forgotten because we will not speak to each other from there to here, but from here to there.

This will encourage another form, the final phase of architecture in terms of representation.

I believe that there will no longer be architecture visible from the exterior . . . [it] will be of no use as people won't be able to see it any more.

On the contrary, what is going to be necessary is a 'decor'; meaning that every home will have a studio with a camera and a television set, through which we will communicate. The final architecture will be the decorative backdrop.

In other words there will be a linked camera which will be the only means of connection to the satellites and other people. There I'll be, sitting in my armchair to talk to my boss, to dad, mum, the kids . . . and so there will be an image, a backdrop; like when you watch a presenter on TV; this backdrop will be the symbolic element, just as architecture before was a symbolic element.

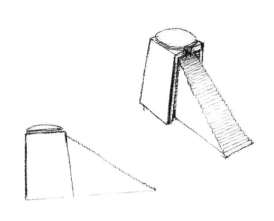

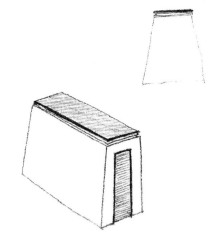

Philippe Starck, 'La rue Starck',
preliminary sketches, 1991

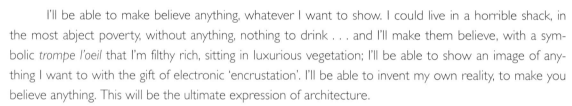

I'll be able to make believe anything, whatever I want to show. I could live in a horrible shack, in the most abject poverty, without anything, nothing to drink . . . and I'll make them believe, with a symbolic *trompe l'oeil* that I'm filthy rich, sitting in luxurious vegetation; I'll be able to show an image of anything I want to with the gift of electronic 'encrustation'. I'll be able to invent my own reality, to make you believe anything. This will be the ultimate expression of architecture.

In terms of representation, architecture has always been a more or less well-made, efficient means of representation, but it's always been that way.

What I would like to be in the future is a seller of catalogues of final images, a producer of those backdrops; they will be diskettes that you put in the machine to make the decor appear in the background; we will live inside them, thanks to interactivity and virtual reality.

The 'worlds' envisaged by Dick and the New Wave of the fifties and sixties have in time left the science fiction ghetto to become widespread social phenomena.

The recent use in everyday life of computers, fax machines, videophones, electronic mail, data banks, bleepers, pagers, portable phones, and the development of a scientific knowledge which can unite the organic and the electronic (biology and technology), is effectively producing a real anthropological mutation.

Frankenstein's dream of creating life (not by chance at the dawn of the industrial civilisation) progresses at great pace thanks to genetic engineering and microelectronics.

The figure of the 'cyborg' (cybernetic organism) is becoming more and more familiar, as is the 'cyberspace' dimension: a sort of virtual reality where the human body and the computer's spatial simulations interact in real time.

New social subjects are born, such as the 'hacker' who, although he belongs to the world of electronic information tries to combat the new powers and spread the information, and the 'cyberpunk', who blends high-tech know-how and pop culture into his own underground version. Starck's operating philosophy appears to make reference to this hybrid, ambiguous, *Blade Runner* inspired dimension.

His vision of a totally artificial world and cities dominated by telecommunication is materialised in the hypothesis of 'La rue Starck', consisting of buildings that don't betray

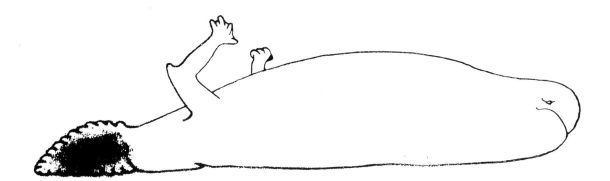

Philippe Starck,
drawing, undated

their functional role on the exterior, and which rise hieratic and like totems on a chequered base: the chequerboard. 'Nani Nani' is joined by 'The Angle', Maison Lemoult, Starck's second house according to a compositional method which follows a theoretically limitless process of addition. The traditional places of the urban landscape (the continuity of vistas, streets, squares, boulevards, great arteries, public and private places) have disappeared, and in their place have appeared the interstices and the 'shadowy areas' between these buildings which are all denoted by a formal remarkableness. It is not the non-dilution of a strongly communicative moment (the monument) within a secondary connecting fabric, but, on the contrary, the grouping together of single buildings of strong visual impact, that confers to 'La rue Starck' a kind of sacredness, typical of a necropolis.

Perhaps the buildings of 'La rue Starck' are none other than the grotesque, magnified version of the images of the post-industrial society: the fax machine, the cellular phone, the computer . . . Like in the Tyrrel Corporation building in *Blade Runner*, nothing of the complexity of the internal functions and activities escapes to the outside and their housing, as for technological objects, follows the rules of styling. But with Starck, the styling, the bodywork can't be simply High Tech or Minimalist because it has to be the scene, the new habitat rich with surprises and emotions for those hybrid characters (the inhabitants of the interstices and the inter-zones) who, having repudiated the sepulchral envelopings of the metaphysical remote controls and virtual realities of presumptuous and stagnant Buddhas, will begin a new, umpteenth voyage: 'on the road again'.

Notes

1. Interview by M di Forti with Philippe Starck in *Il Messaggero*, 4/6/1993.
2. C Colin, *Starck*, Liege/Tubingen, 1989.
3. C Colin, ibid.
4. This extract and the ones that follow are from an interview by Franco Bertoni with Philippe Starck in September 1992.
5. Philip K Dick, *Il Disco di Fiamma*, Milan, 1986, p104 (*Solar Lottery*, Ace Books, 1955).
6. Philip K Dick, *Cacciatore di androidi*, Milan, 1986 (*Blade Runner: Do Androids Dream of Electric Sheep*, Harper Collins, 1972).
7. Philip K Dick *I simulacri*, introduction by C Pagetti, Milan, 1980 (*The Simulacra*, Ace Books, 1964).
8. Interview from 1974 with Philip K Dick 'Psicopatologie neuromantiche', *Più cyber che punk*, Valmerz, Bologna, 1990.
9. 'Declaration of the Surrealist Movement, 27th January 1925', *Surrealist Art*, S Alexandrian, New York, 1970.
10. Philip K Dick, *La svastica sul sole*, Milan, 1983, p40 (*Man in a High Castle*, Penguin, 1993).
11. Philip K Dick, chapter 7, *Our Friends from Frolix 8*, Harper Collins, 1976.
12. Philip K Dick from the conference 'The Android and the Human', Vancouver, 1972.
13. 'Il designer superStarck', *Corriere della Sera*, 23/6/1992.
14. William Gibson, *Neuromante*, Milan, 1986 (*Neuromancer*, Victor Gollancz, 1984).

THE *ARCHITECTURE* **OF PHILIPPE STARCK**

Les Bains-Douches Night Club
7 Rue du Borg L'Abbe
Paris, 1978

The re-adaptation of a building previously used as public baths (Les Bains-Douches) is one of the first tasks Starck undertook as interior designer. He limited himself to a few interventions, keeping the existing mosaics and tiles, and entrusting to this place – fortuitously chosen and anticipating many subsequent emulations equally based on hard and grey tones – the task of conveying 'a Parisian place under the Soviet yoke. I put Soviet writings on the walls. Portraits of Stalin were hung on the walls. A Red Flag was dipped in a pool of blood, onto which was projected the outline of a Doberman in reference to the figure of Stalin.' Starck's orchestration points to the apocalyptic, but real, possibilities of the steel talon and the return of Big Brother ('I wanted to show the opacity, the uncertainty, the isolation of the "done", of indecision and greyness'), and at the same time exorcises the obsessive and infinite melancholy of this hypothesis utilising the setting as a place for celebrating and derision.

L'Élysée Presidential Apartments

55, 56, Rue du Fauburg St Honoré

Paris, 1982

The furnishing of President Mitterand's offices, together with the designs for Madame Mitterand's apartments, was the prestigious assignment which decisively contributed to Starck's affirmation on the international scene, especially in the field of design. From this time onwards, designs and prototypes dating back to the seventies were increasingly put into production by Carte Blanche VIA, Diaform, Baleri Italia, 3 Suisses, XO, Driade . . . with a peak of about sixty objects in production in the space of three years.

It is significant that the Presidential offices offered a prime spot for the prototype of the 'Richard III' club armchair 'in aluminium hand embossed in a helicopter factory' and 'covered in Hermes leather, the richest, the most opulent'.

The resulting environment is described by Starck as 'an austere place – sophisticated lights, grey granite and black marble, pumice stone, drapes and counter-weights – so that a banal gesture becomes theatrical'.

The placement of the prototype for 'Richard III', described by Starck as a dialectical exercise on bourgeoisie typology ('bourgeoisie on the front, but when you turn it around, it's empty; there's a hypocritical side to it that I rather like.') is symptomatic of the client's intelligent 'self-irony' and of Starck's constant, incisive criticism of power and institutions: the emperor is naked.

L'Élysée, Presidential
Apartments, Paris
3 Interior

Café Costes

4-6 Rue Berger, Place des Innocents

Paris, 1984

With Café Costes Starck retraces, after 'Le Bains-Douches' – only this time starting from scratch – the steps on the razor edge of the 'infinite and obsessive melancholy'. The working title of the programme was 'Sad and Beautiful as the Buffet of Prague's Railway Station'. Prague: the city subjugated by the steel talon; the station: the place of arrivals and departures; the buffet: the place in which to wait for the voyage.

Hence the buffet is a submerged place, introverted, set apart from the confusion and the clamour of the station, otherwise like the café in the metropolis.

However, no concession is made to themes such as intimacy or captivating decor. The metaphysical stasis of the buffet is contradicted by the feeling of anxiety that always denotes the wait, and which the environment contributes to increase: the two oversized circular pillars, their pretensions of prowess humiliated by their very utilitarian, basic, housing-estate finish hint at superior structures that don't exist; the staircase does not have a parallel development and widens up towards the area of smaller capacity, where a clock with the wrong hours towers. The skylight is not transparent but illuminated, to increase the claustrophobic sense of the place dominated by the shabby tones of pale grey, green and brown. 'Volumes are quite large and tall, and the materials are humble (although very strong). Everywhere there's emptiness, the coldness of light. A sort of brown uniformity. It's a play of signs.'

With Café Costes Starck stages a show which, like many of his other works, points towards displacement, towards the overturning of the common point of view, towards putting back into play all the things that are taken for granted, with the aim of instilling or provoking new and different behaviour, between objects, objects and people, people and people. That's why the buffet in Prague's station is 'transported' to Paris, where it will live as an alien, that's why it's environment is metaphysical, that's why a place for staying becomes a place for waiting, therefore a place of melancholic and enigmatic tension.

All the symbols left by Starck in the Café Costes are those of the tensions, 'the spleen' that dominated the eighties. This partly explains the extraordinary success of this place, which has become the focus of an international clientele which has obviously recognised itself in this suspended dimension.

Café Costes, Paris
6 View of the first floor

Café Costes, Paris
7 Detail
8 Detail of staircase

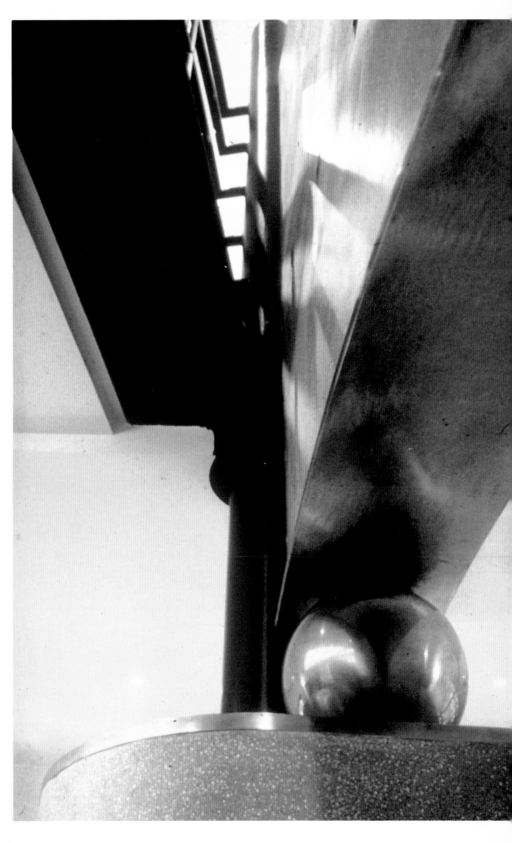

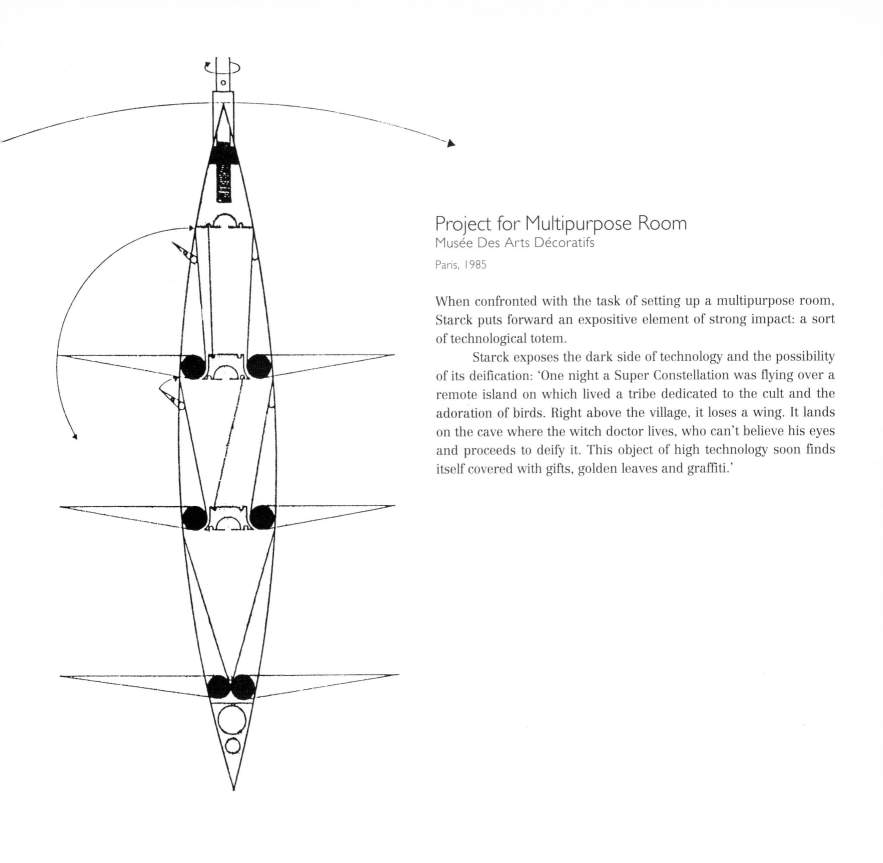

Project for Multipurpose Room
Musée Des Arts Décoratifs

Paris, 1985

When confronted with the task of setting up a multipurpose room, Starck puts forward an expositive element of strong impact: a sort of technological totem.

Starck exposes the dark side of technology and the possibility of its deification: 'One night a Super Constellation was flying over a remote island on which lived a tribe dedicated to the cult and the adoration of birds. Right above the village, it loses a wing. It lands on the cave where the witch doctor lives, who can't believe his eyes and proceeds to deify it. This object of high technology soon finds itself covered with gifts, golden leaves and graffiti.'

Project for Cartier Golden Bridge
Cartier Foundation

Joui en Josas, 1985

Starck, who had worked for Cartier towards the end of the sixties, proposed to replace two footbridges across a river to a small island in the Cartier Foundation park.

The project for the bridge ignores the island which can only be reached by water and cuts diagonally across the river with an entwined metal structure, enamelled with the three colours of the Cartier ring: blue, red and gold.

Furthermore, the bridge plunges like a blade into the water, creating its double, and there is a recess housed on the bridge itself where the landscape is inversely reflected, as in a camera obscura.

An exercise dear to Starck then: on illusion and reality, on true and false, on enigma and double sense.

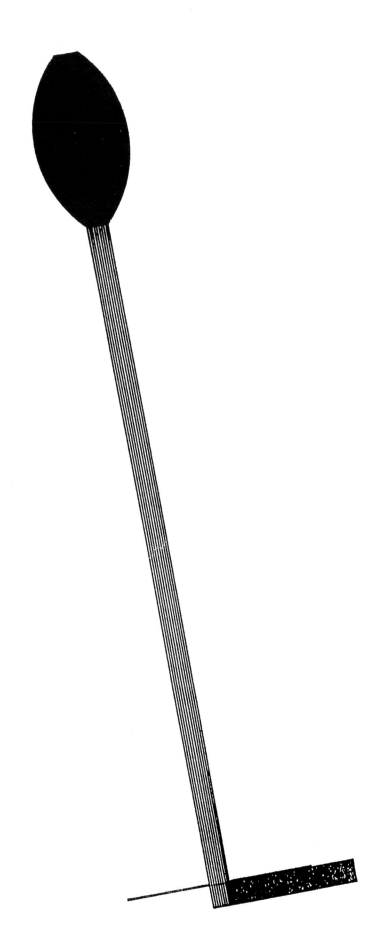

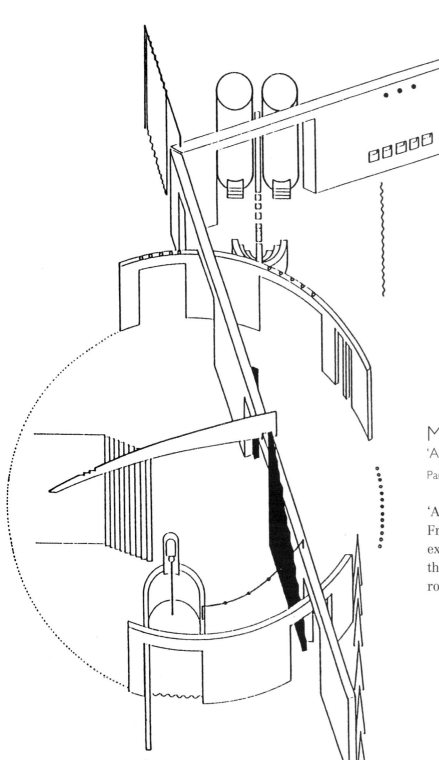

Musée des Monuments Français
'Art et Industrie' Exhibition

Paris, 1985

'A terrible example of fraudulence. An exhibition about the state of French creativity has nothing to exhibit, to the point that it has to exhibit itself. An interesting tension between ancient volumes and this kind of architectural Ariadne's thread running through the rooms.'

Musée des Monuments Français, Paris
12 Design for the installation
of the 'Art et Industrie' Exhibition

Project for Mercedes-Benz Headquarters

Paris, 1986

For this assignment, Starck prepared at least two designs for the front, which retained the two pillars supporting the busts of the company founders, Daimler and Benz, which are evocative of De Chirico. The first design included an arched glazed front reminiscent of paleo-industrial structures, whilst the second, simpler one, is denoted by a green marble finish with apertures staggered against the rigid symmetry of the structure. The company emblem in both cases is subjected to re-design, and assumes the focusing element of silent clock.

The symbolic research continues in the interiors: the black and white chequered display line of the cars ('evoking the race track'), the use of mahogany ('reminiscent of vintage cars' dashboards', and 'evoking Germanism'). Of particular interest are the two mahogany pillars of teardrop section, which are necessary to hide existing structures and contain the preludes to the plastic deformations of structural elements typical of Starck's later works.

Mercedes-Benz
Headquarters, Paris
13 Alternative design
for front elevation
and cross section
14 Plan with elements
in relief

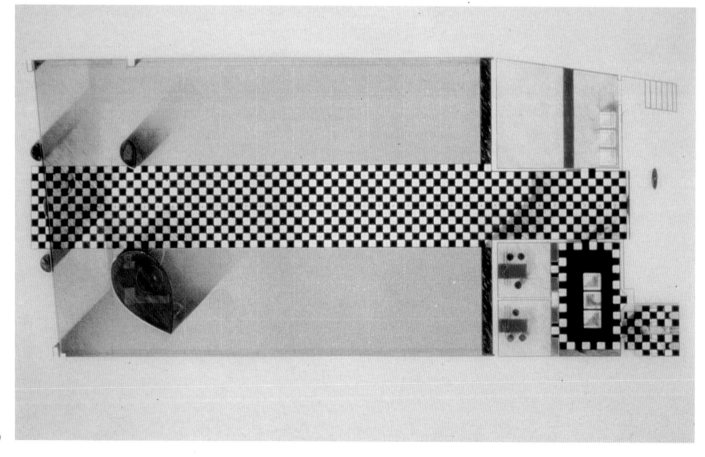

Mercedes-Benz Headquarters, Paris
15 Design for front elevation

Manin Restaurant

2-22-12 Jingudae
Shibuyaku
Tokyo, 1986

'There is nothing here that isn't a symbol, drama or enactment. First of all, an underground location, four floors below street level, a progression towards the depths. A rather vertiginous walkway delineates the definitive break from the outside world. Everything is conceived like an opera. The male actor, the lead role, is the monumental staircase. We arrive at the second actor, the crimson element of drama, a wall three storeys high, padded with red . . . a weighty feminine symbol. The two actors confront each other surrounded by the chorus of the anti-seismic mega-structures.'

Having to plunge into the depths of the earth to create this restaurant/bar, of undoubted similarity to a bunker or an atomic shelter, must have been particularly congenial to Starck, who on this occasion produces one of his most successful stage-set interiors of recent years: a sort of banquet of the survivors. The aerial walkway, almost a ship gangway destined to be removed, marks the definitive cut between the outside world and the environment into which one plunges further, through an oversized staircase, past the bar area. The two vertical connections, more than elements of conjunction, are cutting elements that mark the passages of separation from a real and concrete situation (the outside world) to a situation in which an everyday ritual is consumed within an oneiric and unreal dimension. The ceiling-high red wall padding, the lacquered mahogany finish of walls and ceilings and the diffused light heighten the perception of enclosure and the disproportionate height of the ceiling; all of which is aggravated and rendered more sinister by the ostentatious presence of the black anti-seismic beams which contribute to make the atmosphere even more unnerving.

Manin Restaurant, Tokyo
16 Dining room viewed from above

Manin Restaurant, Tokyo
17 View of anti-seismic structures

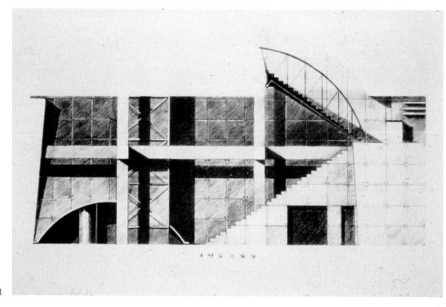

Manin Restaurant, Tokyo
18 Cross section
19 Entrance gangway to the underground restaurant

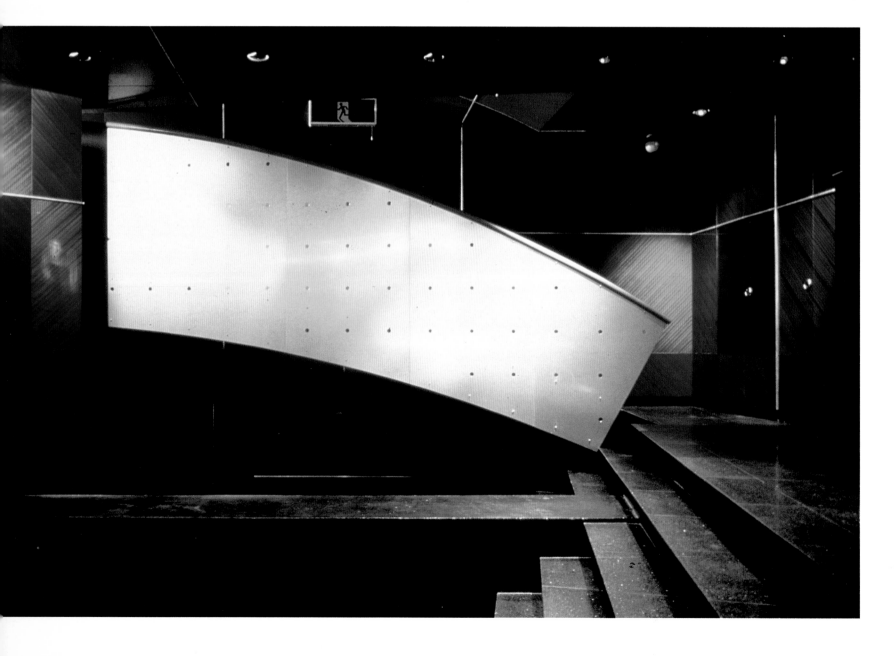

Manin Restaurant,
Tokyo
20 General view

Manin Restaurant, Tokyo
21 Detail of entrance
22 Detail of wall coverings in mahogany,
laquer and padded velvet

Manin Restaurant, Tokyo
23 Detail of staircase
24 Entrance gangway

Project for Starck's First House 'Le Moulin a Vent'

——Montfort-L'Amaury

Paris, 1987

In Starck's first house we again find the search for contradiction and the unnerving symbol. The apparent simplicity of the construction, a squat glass parallelepiped, is contradicted by the oblique cut of the staircase which gives access to a kind of solarium (reminiscent of the Malaparte Villa in Capri) which almost becomes the emerging element of the construction. Starck introduces an element of imbalance into the composition and overthrows the relationship between ground floor and roofing at the total loss of the former, which almost assumes the aspect of a basement. The floor is finished with great black and white checks (in this case the game of chess or draughts, to symbolise the game of life in which it absolutely determines – or not at all – the position in which one finds oneself), and is populated by anthropomorphic, De Chirico-style pillars; the unnerving Muses of the house.

From the starting point, the parallelepiped, Starck arrives at totally different results, in which the overthrow of roles and ubiquity prevail, to the point that he called the building 'Le Moulin a Vent', always still but always in movement.

Starck's First House, project,
Montfort-L'Amaury
25 Axonometric

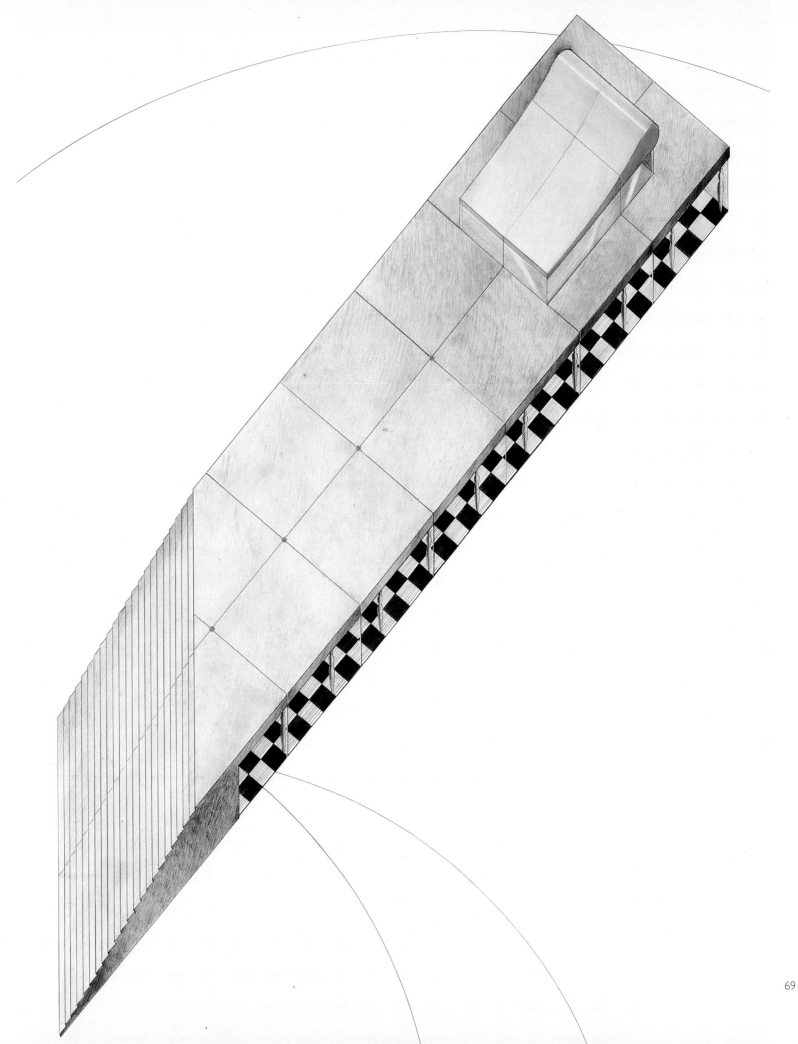

Maison Lemoult 'Le Sphinx'

29 Rue Pierre Poli
92130 Ile Saint Germain
Paris, 1987

The work on the project for Maison Lemoult dates back to 1985, but it was in 1987 that it assumed its definitive form.

'A very difficult assignment: the site is 5.6 metres wide and 60 metres long, with a small budget. Monumentality isn't forgotten: the house is a two-faced Sphinx. It's an out-of-scale work: the apartment is nothing other than a monumental staircase, an intersection of abnormal values'. But Starck gladly accepts the challenge of an abnormality that stimulates him to resume his childhood perversions on *existenzminimum*, and to impose, by contradiction, a strong solution.

The building's levels are split according to Adolf Loos' *Raumplan*, and the building that he designed for Tristan Tzara in Paris, in Avenue Junot, could be cited as amongst the possible antecedents of Maison Lemoult, for its distinctive hierachy.

The front elevation, originally protected by great doors, almost like a piece of furniture (in this respect similar to the '6 Cubes' in Venice, Los Angeles, 1992), is made almost completely of glass: one great oversized window.

Some vertical connecting structures, which were to reach the roof and from there the sky, were never realised. What remains are external staircases with unequal parapets, each leading to a small door, as if reaching for the interior, contradicting the obvious. Perhaps it is necessary to rise and then descend, as in the burial chambers of the Egyptian pyramids. Here again are the themes of descent, of the vertiginous, of the probing of the depths.

The hermetic Sphinx, Maison Lemoult, stretches its paws (the staircases) on the ground, and rests itself, impenetrable and enigmatic.

As a child, in-between plotting ways of torturing my teachers, I was interested in ideas of living space, and I made thousands of drawings to try to find out how to accommodate a family in the minimum amount of square millimetres.

It was lucky for me that I did; without these I would never have been able to conceive the house for the charming Le Moult family on their astonishing site . . . roughly [the size of] an Australian semi-trailer.

Le Moult is clever, sharing my opinion that it is pointless to spend half one's life paying off a house – so he wanted something economical; and to round off the nightmarish brief, being someone of a refined nature, Le Moult also demanded a certain level of architectural quality.

One solution to this could have been to run away. But I couldn't – Le Moult was the first person to have faith in my architecture. I can only thank him for that. And I hope that I have: they now live happily in the biggest little chateau in the world.

Maison Lemoult, Ile Saint Germain
26 Perspective view of facade

Maison Lemoult,
Ile Saint Germain
27 View of facade

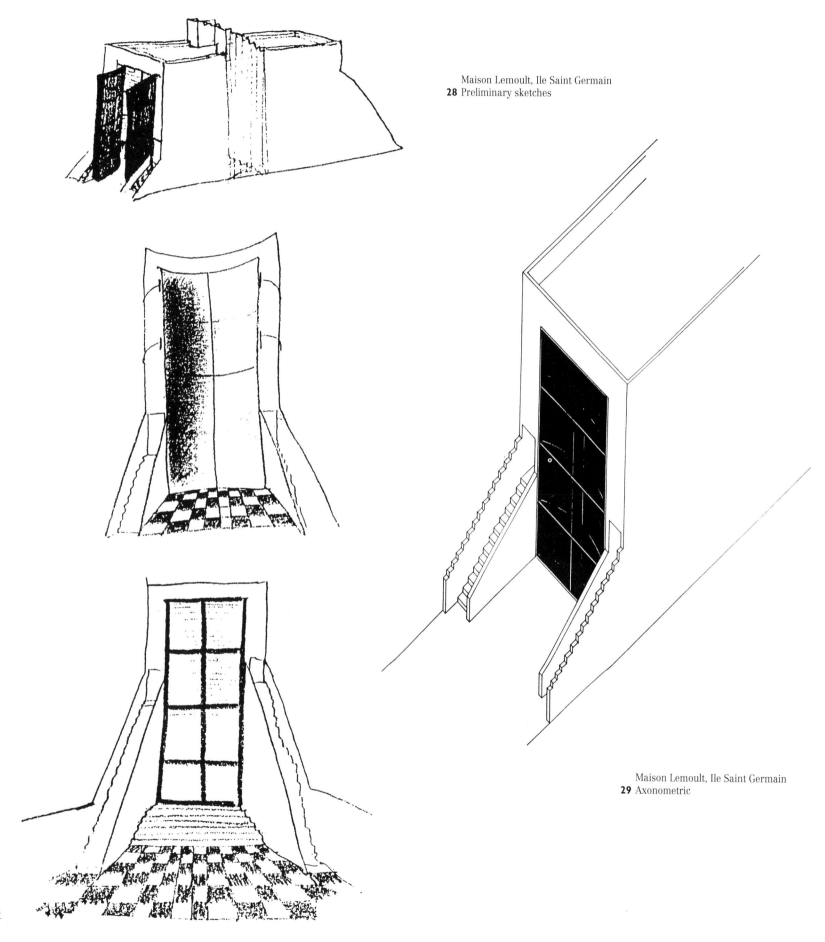

Maison Lemoult, Ile Saint Germain
28 Preliminary sketches

Maison Lemoult, Ile Saint Germain
29 Axonometric

Maison Lemoult, Ile Saint Germain
30 Section

Maison Lemoult, Ile Saint Germain
31 Ground floor plan
32 First floor plan
33 Second floor plan

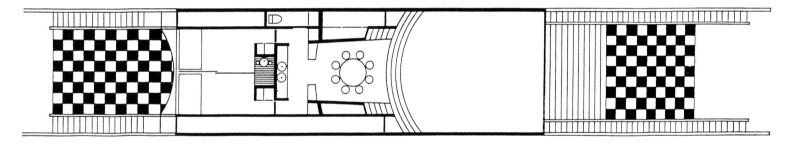

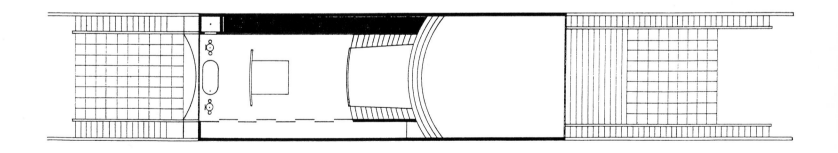

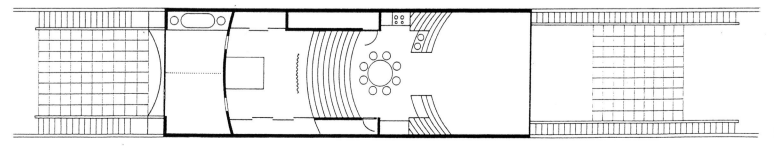

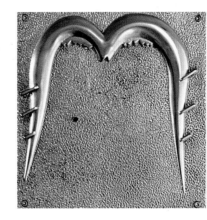

Maison Lemoult, Ile Saint Germain
35 Detail of staircase
36 Switch
37 Bathroom

Maison Lemoult, Ile Saint Germain
34 General view of ground floor

Competition entry for the Tokyo Opera House
(In collaboration with Jean Nouvel)

Tokyo, 1987

'It's the strange object which has come from somewhere else, it's the whale that swallowed Mecca. Object and non-building, huge dimensions, formidable weight, you'd say it was made of solid marble: the weight of a black hole. Inside it, there's only symbol and drama, emotions, great passages – suspended organs like stomachs and livers, an obvious animal reference to emotions. Yes, the order of impressing: the emotional gift that I give people is the gift of living an impressive moment, of experiencing a certain dimension, a weight, almost an anxiety – standing in front of a huge object, beyond comprehension.'

Leaving aside altogether structural, high-tech and contextual notions, Starck and Nouvel propose a building out of all proportion, more than 150 metres tall, vaguely zoomorphic, almost like the trunk of an animal; completely covered with a black material which gives a sinister reflection of the surroundings and the sky, a double that isn't simply a reflection.

The functional spaces float in the gigantic empty interior, in turn impenetrable or connected by staircases and passages of Piranesian inspiration. The unnerving is transformed here in the Kafkaesque anguish of the modern man.

Tokyo Opera House
38 Exterior

Tokyo Opera House
39 Exterior

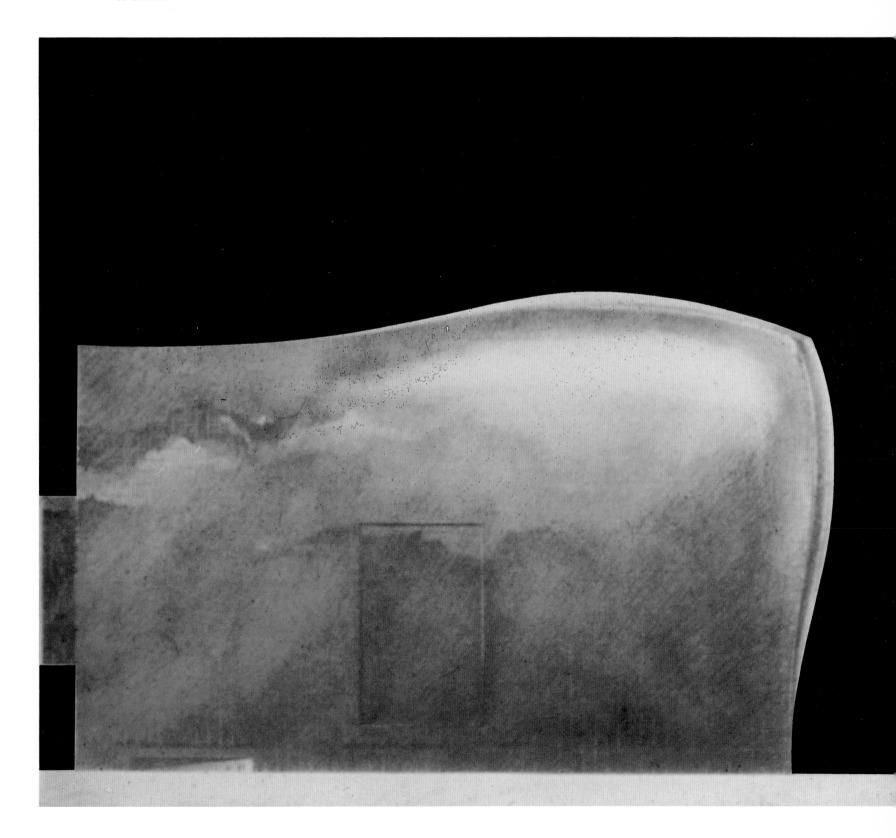

Tokyo Opera House
41 Design for seating
42 Design for chandelier

La Cigale Concert Hall
120 Boulevard Rochechouard
Paris, 1987

'Friendship again; the owners of Les Bains-Douches become film and show producers and buy a historic hall, the first cinema in Paris.' (Program 33: television and theatre studios). Starck intervened mainly in the foyer, which is paved with the chequerboard motif, though, in this case, deformed by the lines leading to the hall and boxes, and finished with an undulating plastic motif reminiscent of Hoffmann (in his Austrian Pavilion at the Paris Exposition of 1925). The ticket booth simulacrum towers in the foyer.

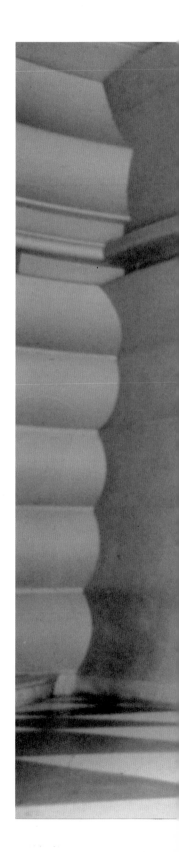

La Cigale Concert Hall, Paris
43 Foyer

La Cigale Concert Hall, Paris
44 Foyer

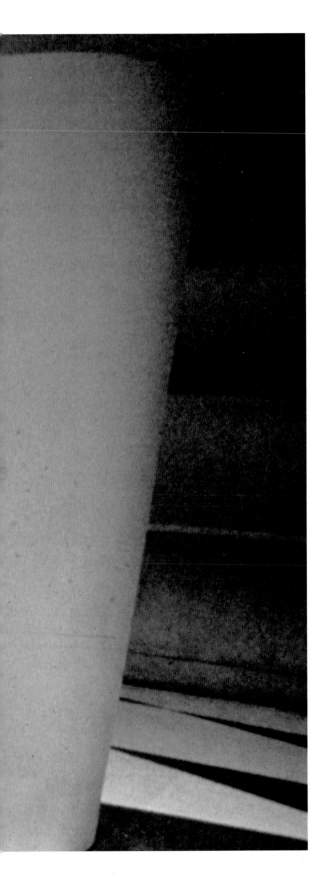

La Cigale Concert Hall, Paris
45 View of the concert hall

Project for the 'Moon Dog' House

Tokyo, 1987

The project for 'Moon Dog', a.k.a. 'la Vie De Betes' ('The Life of Fools') is also a kind of experiment in virtual reality: 'the computer replicates what an animal sees when it enters a house where it dies a death specific to its nature: like a mosquito burning itself on a light bulb, or a chimpanzee splattering against a wall swinging from a liana . . .' The computer's 'reconstruction' was used in a Canal Plus/Channel Four co-production, and won the third 'Oscar' of Monaco's Festival of computer generated images in 1987.

In an 'extra-world' desolate space, dominated by a black, heavy sky speckled with a grid of geometrical luminous points, almost an impalpable but real borderline, Starck imagines a construction symbolic of his bleakest and most hallucinatory concept of the human condition: the nonsense of any action and any effort rendered futile by a terrible and immutable destiny.

The arduous ramp alongside the black and white chequered construction leads up to a howitzer, a kind of primordial science fiction missile. It is Jules Verne's rocket, which should lead to other worlds and expand mankind's horizon. But in the interior the possibility of travel is excluded; on the contrary, there is only the possibility of the contemplation, through the two huge glass walls, of the desolation outside, the sense of anguish reinforced by the interior's void and the abyss beneath.

It is a totally symbolic project, a monument to the vain hopes of escape and evasion, amalgamating Edgar Allan Poe's pit with Philip K Dick's extraterrestrial colonies, in which humans virtually re-enact, through the game of the 'Perky Pat' doll, the experiences of life on Earth.

'Moon Dog – a Dog's Life' Building

The monumental, sculpted concrete stair, with its plant ornamentation topped by a flare of green bronze is a domestic building in the centre of Tokyo. Two intuitive approaches dominate this project. The first is the need which an inhabitant has for an emotional relationship with his/her place of shelter. In order to achieve this the building's unique silhouette enables the person to recognise the house from afar, and even in the street context a link begins to forge itself that will unite inhabitant and building – a link that will be reinforced by the notion of territory created by the stairs dominating the building's facade. The other more symbolic approach is that of the quest for poetic space – a legacy left by failed Utopias. It is moving to see in some of the illustrations to Jules Verne's books to what extent so many of the guiding intuitions in these stories were intrinsically right, but how fragile they became in the voyage through the history of form.

The 'Moon Dog' building in Tokyo will attempt to express the poetry that lies in the flaws of human dreams.

Project for the 'Moon Dog' House, Tokyo
46 Preliminary sketch

Project for the 'Moon Dog' House, Tokyo
47 Preliminary sketch
48 Computer graphic of exterior

Project for the 'Moon Dog' House, Tokyo
49 Computer graphic showing view from above
50 Computer graphic of exterior

Project for the 'Moon Dog' House, Tokyo
51 Computer graphic, exterior detail

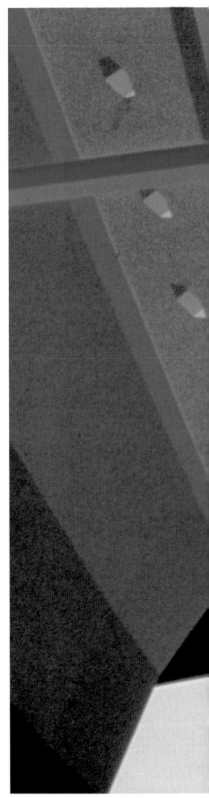

Project for the 'Moon Dog' House, Tokyo
52 Computer graphic, interior view

Project for the 'Moon Dog' House, Tokyo
53 Computer graphic, interior view

Laguiole Knife Factory

ZA Route d'Aubrac
12210 Laguiole
France, 1988

Three fundamental elements – the parallelepiped of the factory, covered in steel, the most appropriate material considering the product, and its glass front, through which are visible the 'M (Serie Lang)' display tables, with legs shaped like a knife blade; the meta-physical chequerboard on the courtyard; and above all, the gigantic blade jutting out from the building – are images altogether surreal and symbolic.

Jean-Luis Costes, of the Café Costes in Paris, loves his country, architecture and me – and I, myself, love him too.

This is why I willingly accepted his offer to construct (with a subsidy from the local government) a factory producing knives that are so symbolic of our beloved France.

The factory, which is situated amidst magnificent mountains, had to be economical and had to make use of local resources. Above all, it had to have a powerful image.

What I find interesting is the idea that architecture has no need of charity to survive and prosper if it can help industry and commerce in a dignified manner. Moreover, I think that architecture can actually help an industry's reputation and, by helping in this way, it no longer has a need of a cultural pretext to find the necessary subsidies for its realisation.

The Laguiole factory, with its shining blade, is the beginning of my proposal.

Laguiole Knife Factory
54 Preliminary sketches

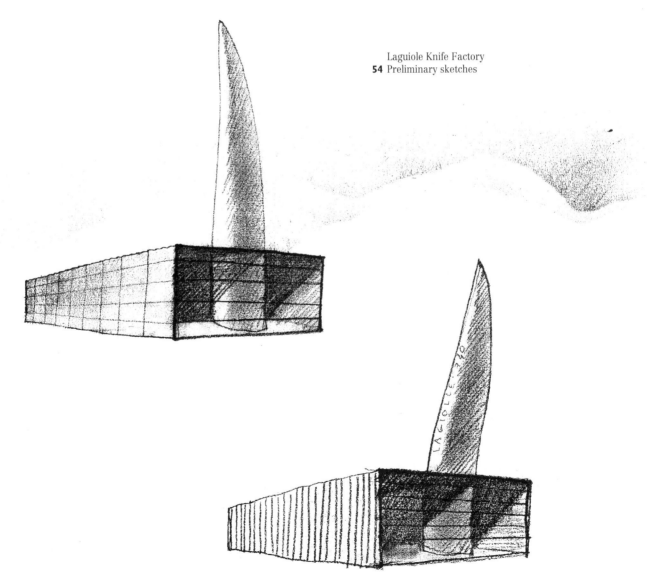

Laguiole
Knife Factory
55 Side elevation

Laguiole Knife Factory
56 Preliminary sketches

Laguiole Knife Factory
57 Overall view of factory

Café Mystique

6-27-8 Jingumae
Shibuja-Ku

Tokyo, 1988

'A project that developed from a new kind of logic as starting point: an esoteric sign found in a book bought from a witch in Formentera. Behind this there is always the idea of miracles, of mysteries.'

Starck places the witch's enigmatic sign on the slightly convex entrance door, almost to express a pulsating tension coming from within, and has it scored by thin lines similar to those of music sheets, on which the symbol assumes the aspect of a musical note. Starck matches Japanese Zen with Mediterranean mystery.

In the interior there are interventions: furnishings, redesigned details, but above all, in characteristically contradictory spirit, the presentation of symbols typical of the consumer society (the Playboy Bunny, the Coca-Cola device, the logo on the Dr Glob chair . . .) in the style of prehistoric murals.

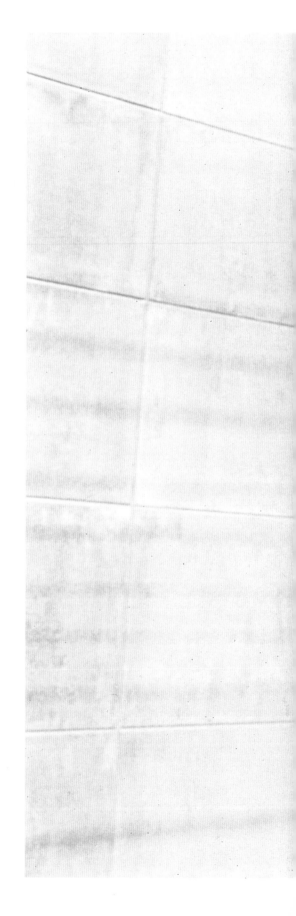

Café Mystique, Tokyo
58 Entrance

Café Mystique, Tokyo
59 Interior showing freize

Café Mystique, Tokyo
60 Interior

Royalton Hotel

44 West 44th Street

New York, 1988

The work of restructuring the Royalton gave Starck little possibility for expression from an architectural point of view, and forced him to concentrate on decor and furniture, to which he dedicated himself with the skill of a magician, always able to surprise, relying mainly on his abilities as a designer.

Royalton Hotel,
New York
62 Front facade

Royalton Hotel,
New York
63 Detail of entrance
64 Reading room

Royalton Hotel, New York
65 Detail of interior

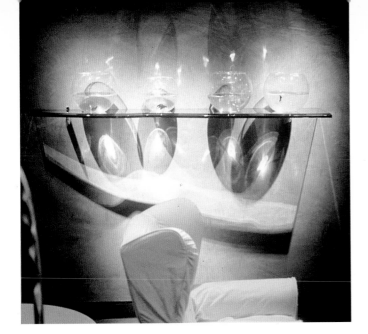

Royalton Hotel, New York
66 Detail of shelf
67 Breakfast room

Royalton Hotel, New York
70 Interior of guest room

Royalton Hotel, New York
68 Design for guest room
69 Design for guest room

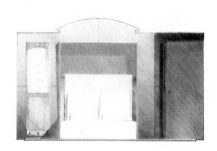

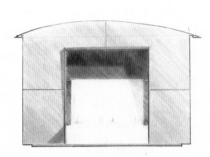

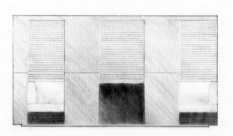

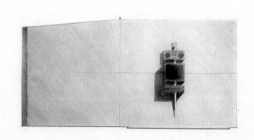

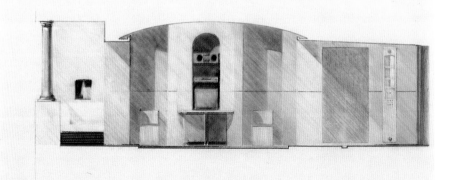

Asahi 'La Flamme'

Azumabashi 1-25-4-7-9
Sumida-Ku
Tokyo, 1989

The three themes evoked by Starck – energy, mystery and passion – although appropriate to his poetry and to this work, with its appearance of a precious casket, a prelude to the unveiling of supernatural mysteries, are yet insufficient to explain this successful architecture of many languages. The suggestions can be numerous and varied: from the unnerving monolith of *2001: A Space Odyssey*, to the disproportionate scale of a surrealist object/sculpture, but the most appropriate would appear to be the 'Rex' ocean liner ploughing the waves through the night in Fellini's *Amarcord*. 'La Flamme' is a night liner, dotted with the lights escaping from its port-holes.

The luminous base hints at detachment from its location, from Earth: its place is nowhere.

It is a ubiquitous building that could move or be moved in any of the *Blade Runner* metropolises: San Francisco, New York, London; its temporary mooring in Tokyo is by chance.

The 'Flamme', the golden teardrop on its summit, with its appearance of sail, or rudder, or smoke from the funnel, dominates the surrounding urban landscape like an ancient dome, and through its utter lack of purpose sublimates the feeling of estrangement imposed by the building, calling for the awareness of now forgotten dimensions such as purposelessness, play, passion. The docking of Asahi in the metropolis translates Philip K Dick's need for an encounter with extraterrestrial entities, with whom, he thought, he would have felt more affinity and harmony than with the neighbours.

In the interior, which is almost completely padded (to muffle the outside noise) and lined with rows of ropes and portholes, the themes of futuristic ships are to be found again: the bridge and the stairs leading up to the deck, the corridors, the services, the holds; all populated with pillars swollen by their task or by an interior life that makes them resemble post-bomb bacilli.

Asahi is the sailing ship of the year 2500, transporting a new humanity. But if it's true that science fiction always, in any case, deals with the present, and that the work of art isn't so much produced for posterity as to render justice to the past and the present, then Asahi represents one of the needs for posterity of our time, between Utopia and end of millennium new sensitivity.

A black polished granite urn upon a luminous glass staircase is topped by a 'flame', covered in matt gold. The aim of this building when completed, not far from the Asakusa Temple, will be to gather together young creative Japanese, giving them the means for research as well as practical skills. It is drawn in an essentially symbolic spirit. Here, the luminous base plays with energy and the urn with mystery, while the flame states this is a place of passion. This building is the first important pawn in the war staged between large Japanese firms through architecture.

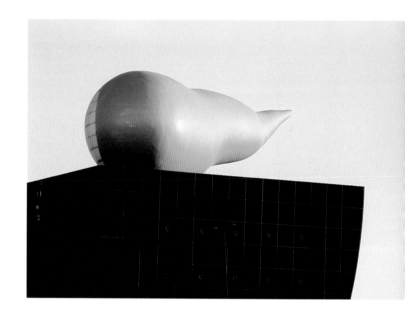

Asahi, Tokyo
71 Detail of 'flame' on the roof
72 View of exterior

Asahi, Tokyo
73 Roofing
74 Exterior, detail of steps

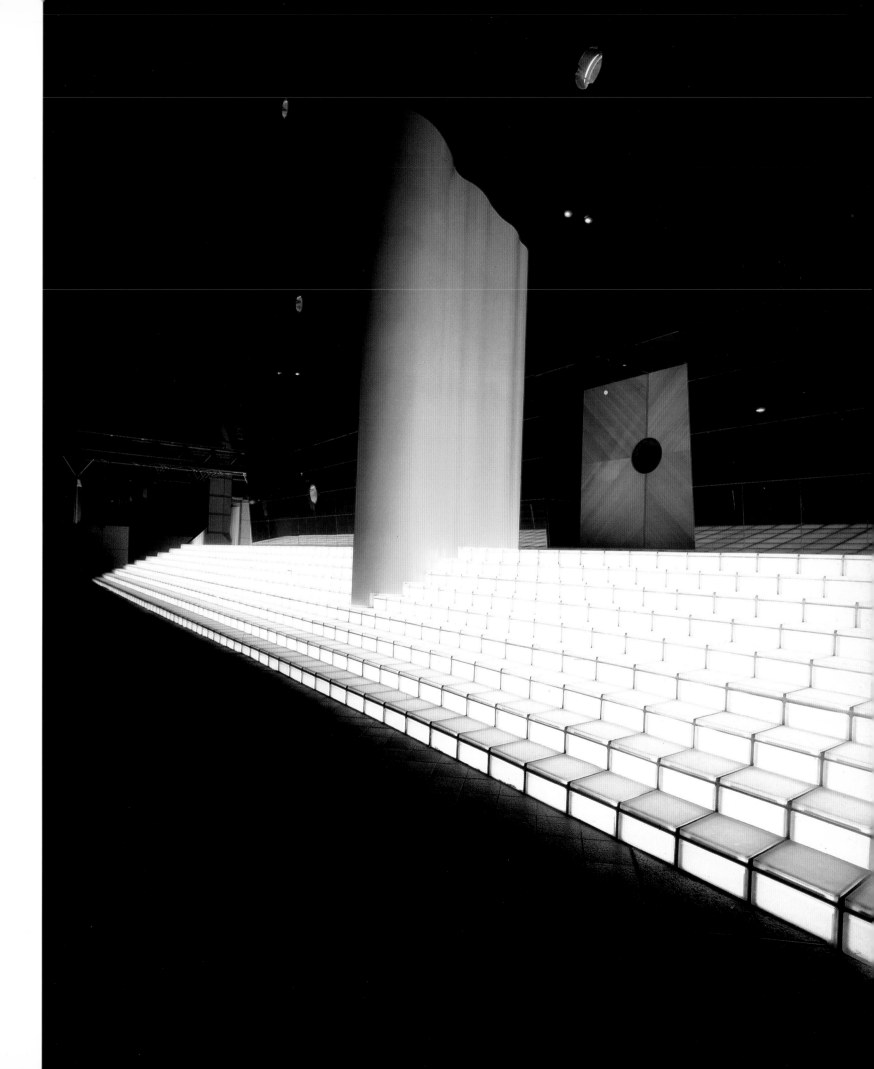

Asahi, Tokyo
75 Design for front elevation
76 Staircase joining first and second floors

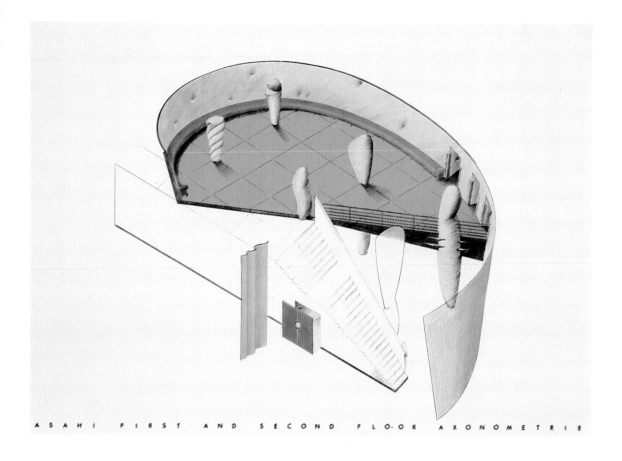

ASAHI FIRST AND SECOND FLOOR AXONOMETRIE

Asahi, Tokyo
77 Axonometric of first
and second floors
78 Axonometric of fourth
and fifth floors
79 First floor, interior

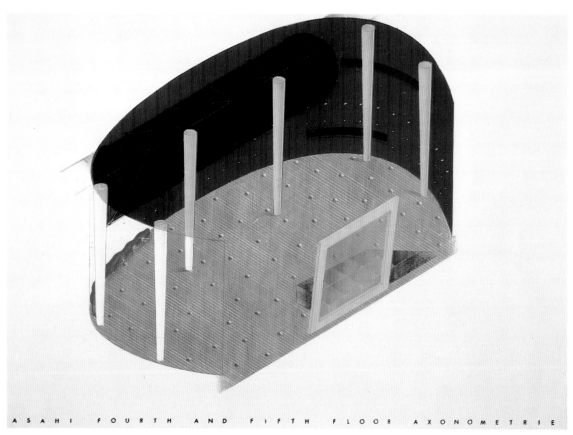

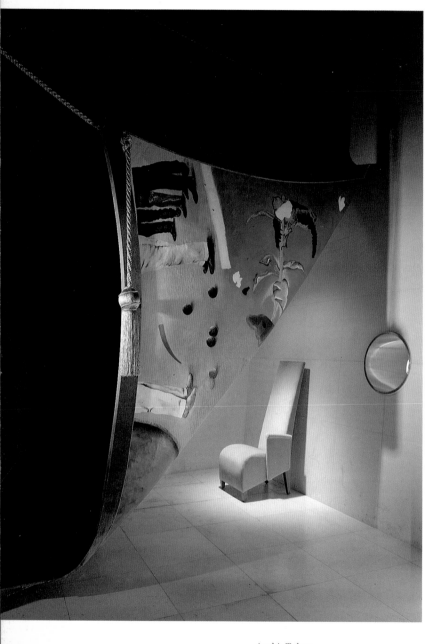

Asahi, Tokyo
80 Detail of first floor interior
81 First floor interior

Asahi, Tokyo
82 Second floor interior
83 Second floor interior

Multipurpose Building 'Nani Nani'

Shirokane Dai 4-273-42
Minato Ku
Tokyo, 1989

'The building was originally called "Godzilla" after a mythical monster which lives beneath the waves, like the Loch Ness monster, a very Japanese metaphor which today, as is very clear in films, represents the atomic bomb. I like to see the building as a fort, the ultimate shelter against the dangers waiting for us around the corner, just as I find the symbolism in "Godzilla" interesting.

After I decided to cover it with oxidised copper, it became the Green Monster of Bayou: green not through choice of colour but of a material which is in perpetual transformation and self-destruction. The Green Monster of Bayou is Louisiana folklore: it's a monster made up of all the human bodies thrown in the swamp that live again by becoming a man eating monster, a little like werewolves.'

The building undoubtedly makes zoomorphic references, as testified by a few of the preliminary sketches: the head of an unknown being emerges from the depths of the earth to observe the urban scene.

The ribs on the summit and on the vertical walls, once the original proposal for a vertiginous, lit staircase are reminiscent of a covering of scales.

Gaudi and Mendelsohn could be cited as some of the possible antecedents of this work, the former for the reptilian-like roofing of the Calvet and Battlo houses, the latter for the Einstein Tower in Potsdam.

But almost a century later the fears of an anthropological mutation taking place and of a possible impending apocalyptic end have become a certainty. The reactions can no longer be the spiritual introspection of Gaudi or Mendelsohn's expressionist shout: the only possible thing to do, Starck appears to say, is to try and live together with the new monsters.

The word 'Naninani' means the unnameable, that which cannot be named. It is a Japanese word cried out by a person on seeing a ghost. The 'Nani Nani' building is worthy of its name: it is a biomorphic 'monster' in bronze, with green oxidised bronze trickling down its sides – a building that issues from the very depths of Japanese subconscious fears.

The 'Nani Nani' building attempts to respond to that age-old question: 'Do inanimate objects have a soul?' Perhaps 'Nani Nani' does have a soul; in any case, it is the first living building. The oxidised green with which it is made continually trickles down to the ground where it will gradually make tiny intricate, intertwining fissures; and, over the years, these will form the many roots which will reveal the organic development of this building . . . in which you shouldn't stay alone at night . . .

'Nani Nani', Tokyo
84 Detail of roofing
85 Side elevation

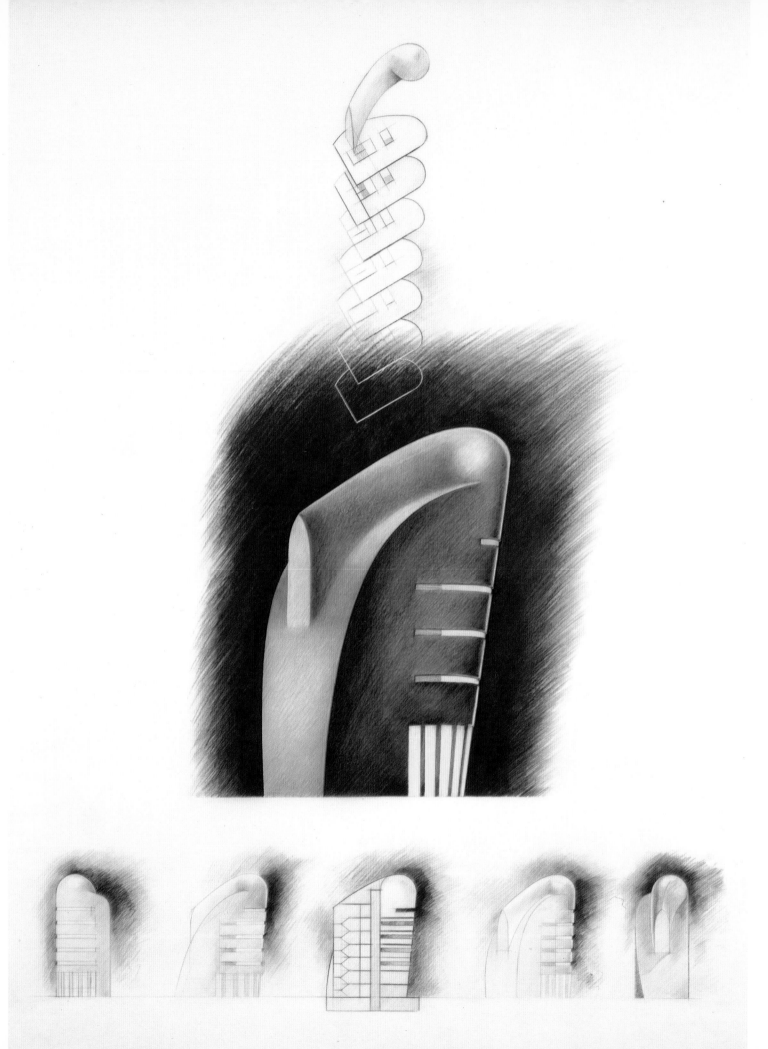

'Nani Nani', Tokyo
86 Elevations, sections and isometric
87 Overall view of exterior

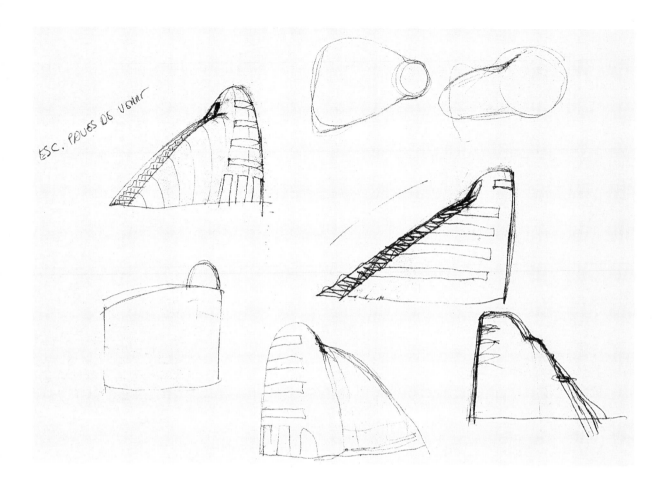

ESC. PADAS DE VIDRO

'Nani Nani', Tokyo
88 Preliminary sketches
89 Preliminary sketches

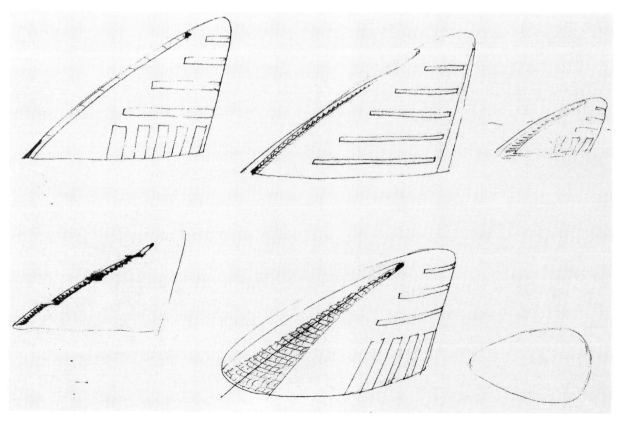

'Nani Nani', Tokyo
90 Preliminary sketches
91 Preliminary sketches

'Nani Nani', Tokyo
92 Preliminary sketches

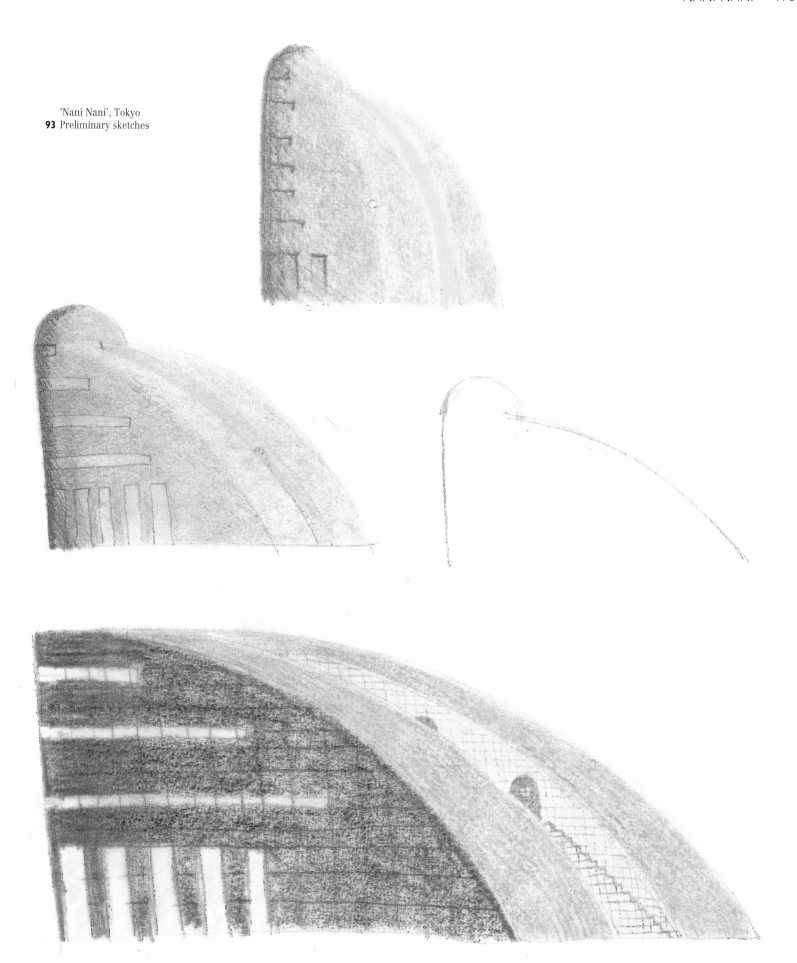

'Nani Nani', Tokyo
93 Preliminary sketches

'Nani Nani', Tokyo
94 Computer graphic of structure
95 Computer graphics of exterior

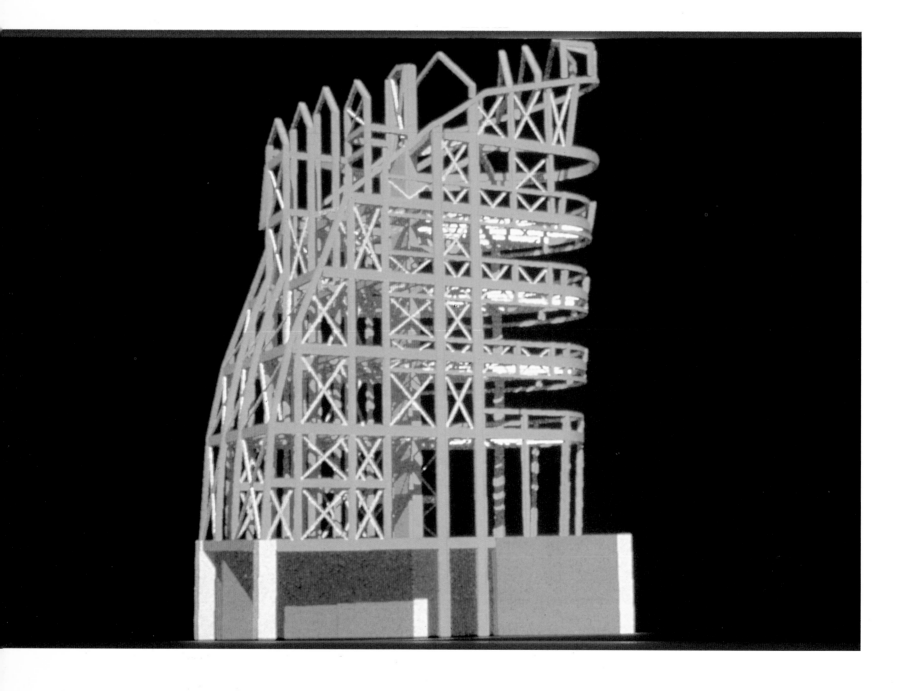

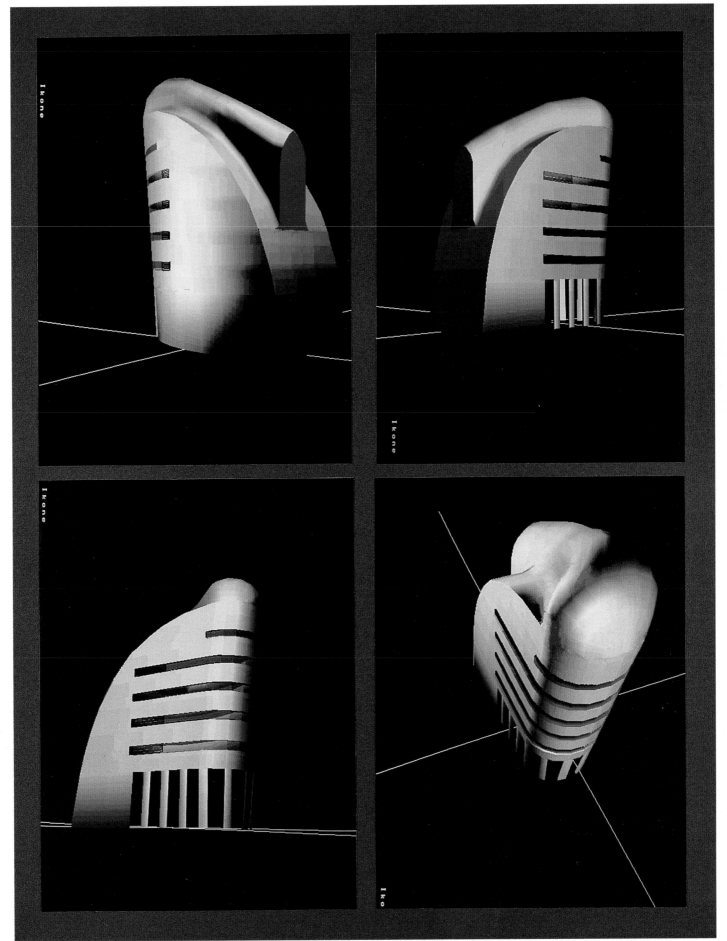

Salone Coppola

Corso Garibaldi 110
Milan, 1989

In this architecture of interiors for hairstylist Coppola, Starck proposes again, in opportune measures, some of the *leit-motifs* of his production – the passage from the darkened entrance to the luminous booths (almost places for initiation and transformation, but with a streak of irony) via a staircase with unequal parapets, as in Maison Lemoult, and the banister that seems to emerge and disappear into the wall – almost as if always wanting to break from the banal, the taken for granted, to discover in all things and all actions, no matter how small, the potential for diversity.

Salone Coppola, Milan
96 Decorative detail
97 Entrance

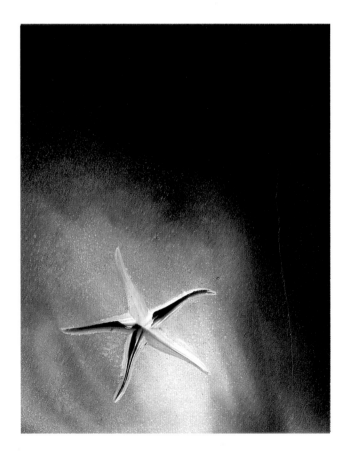

Salone Coppola, Milan
98 Salon cubicles

Salone Coppola, Milan
99 Detail of staircase banister
100 Access staircase to salon

Salone Coppola, Milan
101 Detail of entrance
102 Interior

Teatriz Restaurant

Hermosilla 15
Madrid, 1990

The declared reason for most of Starck's production as designer and architect is to surprise, to call for pause and reflection, so that, stimulated by the empathic force of the objects, everyone can glimpse the possibility of another way of living and behaving: 'My interlocutor must be able to say: "If a toothbrush can be like this, imagine how my life could be!"'

Teatriz is the appointed place for this dimension, impregnated with symbols. The theme is the conversion of a theatre to a restaurant. The dining room occupies the stalls: the spectators become the protagonists. On the stage, partially protected by a semi-transparent curtain, is the monolithic presence of the onyx luminous bar, and a huge mirror reflecting life in the dining room.

The direct connection of the stalls and the stage by means of a flight of steps allows all the diners, in their journeys to and from the bar, to assume the unusual role of actors, emphasised by an out of the ordinary scenography.

Ambiguity still remains, although far removed from Bunuel's nightmare of the meal on stage in *The Discreet Charm of the Bourgeoisie*. On the floor of the restaurant there is an inlaid depiction of De Chirico's *The Two Sisters* of 1915, as a tribute to the master of enigma.

An enormous black pleated drape enveloping the restaurant only opens with the aid of a Daliesque crutch, to reveal a small room on the first floor, as if to indicate that there are always other curtains to tear or pull back.

For Starck 'It's the first time that I've reached a perfect balance of the parameters of fantasy, rigour and empathy. The powerful idea, which is new to me, is that it is possible to achieve strong emotions within the confines of a friendly disposition, that it is possible to achieve fantasy without giving up rigour, that it is possible to achieve ambiguous places that still remain elegant.'

The general layout is straightforward: in the hallway the rigorously chequered floor and the bacilliform pillars (like those in Asahi), are suspended in a rarefied atmosphere; then comes the waiting area that leads into the dining room or, through a corridor, to the bar. On the floor below there's the 'Conspirator's Bar', a pub/disco.

Teatriz Restaurant, Madrid
103 Detail of entrance pillars
104 Entrance

Teatriz Restaurant, Madrid
105 Plan
106 Access corridors to washrooms
with luminous panels

Scattered everywhere are the signs of role reversals and the surprise effect: the baroque and exuberantly ornamental tables are used as basins in the washrooms, but in the first floor bar they return to their intended function; the toilet cubicles are hermetically sealed by a metal door, in a completely tiled, sinisterly lit environment; the basement saloon has an iridescent intimacy, (there's even a boiserie) revealed by its reflection in the wall mirror with a half-raised black curtain; and the luminous panels along the corridor running adjacent to the restaurant hint at moments of the life outside despite their pallor.

Teatriz is the place for ubiquity: where one can be in many places at once, assume different roles, be incapable of distinguishing between illusion and reality, where the views are mutable and interchangeable, a place where as Philip K Dick would put it, nobody would be surprised 'to meet Mini . . . a small man, who wore a traditional cut jacket resplendent with purple Ionic snake skin, with a sparkling cummerbund and Brazilian pig skin shoes with upturned tips', and to find out that 'Mini looked exactly like what he was: a dried fruit wholesaler.'

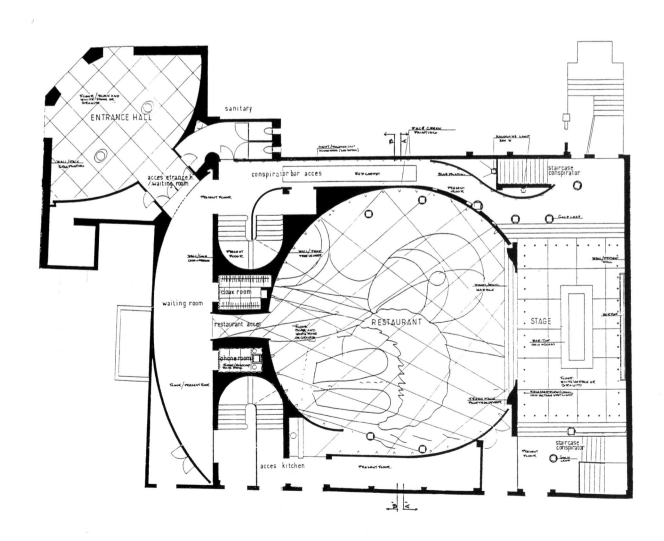

Teatriz Restaurant, Madrid
107 View of the bar from the restaurant
108 Detail of open drapes over the dining room

Teatriz Restaurant, Madrid
110 Basement bar
111 Drapes surrounding dining room

Teatriz Restaurant, Madrid
109 View of the bar from the restaurant

Teatriz Restaurant, Madrid
112 Dining room floor (based on Giorgio de Chirico)
113 View of dining room

Teatriz Restaurant, Madrid
114 Detail of table
115 Detail of appliqué

Teatriz Restaurant, Madrid
116 Entrance to basement room

Teatriz Restaurant, Madrid
117 Washroom, detail
118 Washroom, corridor

Teatriz Restaurant, Madrid
119 Washroom, basin
120 Washroom, toilet cubicles

French Pavilion, Venice Biennale
121 Model in bronze

French Pavilion at the Venice Biennale
Project

1990

'This box has been so filled with French spirit that in the end it tilts and becomes Venetian.' Thus Starck summarises the presence of France in the Biennale gardens.

The pavilion has a trapezoidal base and is tilted to one side, as if its north and east sides are sinking into the waters of the nearby St Elena Canal. There is even a flight of steps going from the north side towards the waters of the canal.

The interior is organised on three levels: the services, the dropping-off area at ground level and a raised platform.

The various floors are connected by means of stairs and even on the outside, on the east side, by a sort of elevator with a fin-shaped base. The proposal for direct access from the canal to the dropping-off areas and the exhibition rooms is an intelligent one, considering the means of transport in the Lagoon.

The tall and narrow apertures on the sides of the edifice are protected by bronze doors which look like rudders, and which don't open on hinges, but oscillate on the base or at the apex.

Natural and artificial light both come from above, filtered by a false ceiling. At night, the light from the inside floods the darkness inclined at an angle.

As a tribute to Venice, the edifice has a terrestrial life and an aquatic life, is hermetically sealed from the outside, and has a privileged rapport with the two Venetian elements which have caused so much passion within the ouevre of topographical painting for centuries: water and sky.

These elements are not incorporated naturalistically or descriptively though, but paraphrase Starck himself, as significant symbols of a condition: 'Feet in the mud and head in the sky'.

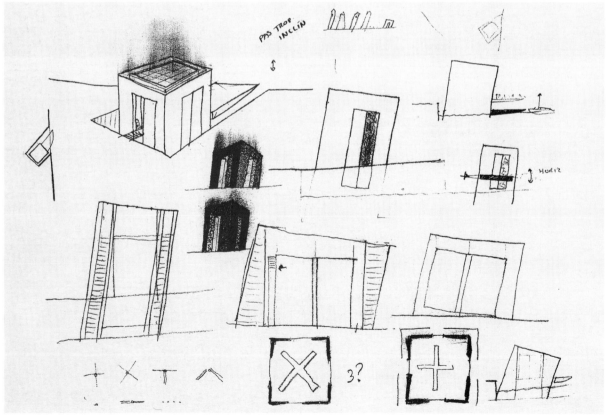

French Pavilion,
Venice Biennale
122 Preliminary sketches
123 Preliminary sketches

French Pavilion,
Venice Biennale
124 Plans

French Pavilion,
Venice Biennale
125 Model
126 Model

French Pavilion,
Venice Biennale
127 North side and section

French Pavilion,
Venice Biennale
128 South side and section

FACADESUD

French Pavilion,
Venice Biennale
129 West side and section
130 East side and section

'Le Baron Vert' Office Building

Tanimachi 9-5-1
Chuo-Ku
Osaka, 1990

Like its twin 'Le Baron Rouge', still under construction, 'Le Baron Vert' perhaps constitutes the highest example of Starck's architectural and symbolic synthesis.

A companion to the descriptive exuberance of Teatriz and the Royalton Hotel, 'Le Baron Vert' re-employs the tension ever present in Starck between a technical and expressive synthesis that here finds its crowning glory.

The memory of the knife blade that cuts the sky of Laguiole, of the 'Ray Menta' lamp ('the coitus of a mega-rotor with a space solar panel'), of cutting as a gesture to discover and unveil what hides behind appearances, and the wish to surprise, are summarised and translated into an architectural style less descriptive and 'naturalistic' than others, and certainly more absolute.

The construction in reinforced concrete is clad with varnished metallic panels which accentuate its lightness, almost like the work of an aeronautical factory, and the face is slit by seven 'cuts' which, as in Lucio Fontana's paintings, make the surface bend when it reacts to the stimulus received. The cuts become the windows, which run the entire length of the floors. The trick of tilting the glass towards the inside renders them even more mimetic.

What remains in 'Le Baron Vert' is the poetry of the disorienting and out of proportion object, of the negation of perpendicularity in favour of a trapezoidal form narrowing towards the top; of the impossibility, because 'it comes from the extra-world', of the dialogue between the building and its surroundings; of the strong affirmation of its identity as an alien – but in a rare synthesis of visual impact with minimal expressive means.

'Le Baron Vert', Osaka
131 Front elevation
132 Detail of exterior

'Le Baron Vert', Osaka
133 General view
134 General view

'Le Baron Vert', Osaka
135 Entrance
136 Front elevation, detail

'Le Baron Vert', Osaka
137 Interior

'Le Baron Vert', Osaka
138 Interior detail and window

'Le Baron Vert', Osaka
139 Washroom
140 Interior

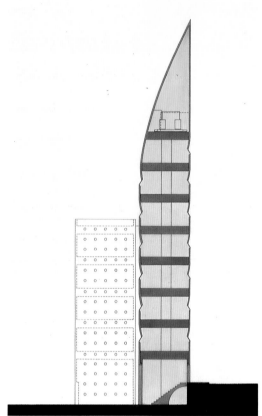

'Le Baron Rouge', Osaka
141 Longitudinal section
142 Transversal section
143 Design for window section

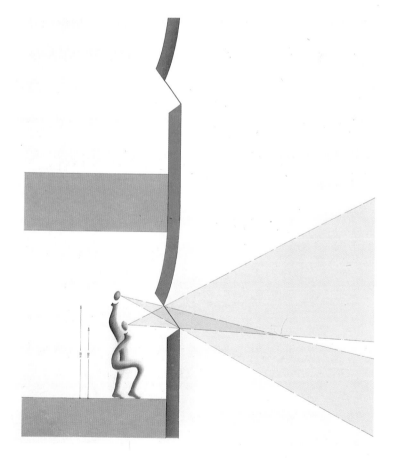

'Le Baron Rouge', Osaka
144 Design for front elevation

MEISEI OSAKA STARCK

Paramount Hotel

235 West 46th Street
New York, 1990

In the Paramount, after the Royalton, we witness Starck's display of a myriad of solutions, which he extracts endlessly and tirelessly from his compositive and decorative baggage, when constricted to using a pre-existing building.

With the Paramount, Starck intended to realise the paradox of 'the democracy of *haute couture*' and make the most diverse social stratas feel equally welcome: 'The youth, the unknown artist, the old university maths professor'.

Three areas form the prelude to the 'luxury Babel' of the six hundred and ten bedrooms: the entrance, the lobby, and the mezzanine meeting place. The entrance, the walls of which are covered with marble slabs from which red roses peek out, gives access to the lobby which is dominated by the staircase leading up to the mezzanine room. The staircase widens as it rises and is flanked on one side by a golden wall with a sharp, curved banister running alongside it, and on the other by a glass parapet which cuts the steps lengthways, rendering the external side of the steps unusable, almost as if the necessity for protection and its course were developed as an afterthought.

In the lobby, the calculatedly different pieces of furnishing rest on a widely chequered carpet, rotated according to the perimeter walls. The mezzanine meeting room opens on the lobby like a row of theatre tiers.

No detail has been spared in the various other environments and rooms: from the mirror indicating the temperature outside to the eye-shaped television cabinet, from the postcard stand to the bathroom waste baskets, from the ironic distorting mirrors to the corner protectors (a separating rod that terminates in a shape which lovingly embraces the wall's corner, usually so detested).

Paramount Hotel, New York
145 Detail of entrance wall
146 Facade and entrance

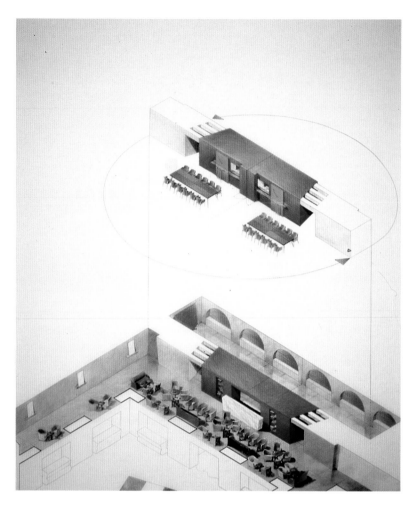

Paramount Hotel, New York
147 Cut away axonometric of hall
148 Perspectives of mezzanine lobby

Paramount Hotel, New York
149 Axonometric of hall

STARCK

Paramount Hotel, New York
150 Mezzanine
151 Hall

Paramount Hotel, New York
152 Detail of hall staircase
153 Detail of staircase

Paramount Hotel, New York
154 Top of corner protector

Paramount Hotel, New York
155 Corner protector

Paramount Hotel, New York
156 Corridor
157 Conference room on mezzanine

Project for the École des Beaux Arts
(Competition entry in collaboration with Luc Arsène-Henry jr)
La Villette Basin
Paris, 1991

Starck's working title for the text accompanying the blueprints is 'The Fertile Surprises', and he assigns to the blueprints the task of 'exploring the effective possibilities of an intuitive city, composed of *émouvant* objects that don't induce the passer-by to reflection through their inherent quality of building, but rather through their rich and open imagery, which opens doors on the work; of creating, through an enactment of these fertile surprises not spectators, but creators of their own life.'

The presence of the canal in the area of La Villette Basin defined by the contract, stimulated Starck to enhance the dichotomy between the two blocks of building which are practically truncated by the stretch of water right from the preliminary sketches. The first ideas explore the contraposition of two upturned truncated cones, vertically sectioned, and the duplication of two trapezoids in which the offset rising lines of the floors are inverted. The constant factor is the building's elevation on an ample luminous platform, as in Asahi.

These ideas were eventually put aside in favour of studies for two different buildings encapsulated in an identical glass structure.

The Medusa vision to which Starck refers in defining this work is necessary to measure the strongly communicative architecture of the internal structures, by means of a total vision that is not stylistically characterised, and that doesn't allow one to see directly but only to perceive the life that takes place inside the school.

The building is divided into two blocks on the opposite banks of the canal which are connected by a room under the canal itself. The building for the first cycle of studies is convex and distinguished by a great arch, clearly making reference to the themes of entry and passage, as well as those of openness and availability. In the second building, destined for the final courses, the development of the staircase around the cylindrical structure hints at a kind Tower of Babel: to the elevation of knowledge.

Both the buildings, although dissimilar, are encapsulated within two identical glass parallelepipeds, which confer the appearance of aquariums to the two school blocks.

This image makes clear reference to the themes of water and the canal running beneath, but also to a significant overturning of

Our society today, more than ever before, needs *active* members; not just people who seem to be working, but people in control of their abilities, who work to make something of and transform our civilisation. The school is one of the most important means of the evolution of this type of work and this type of person; and this is why we have attempted, in turn, not to make a school that merely seems like a school, but one that is a genuinely active tool producing not 'extras' but 'actors'.

These days we are all submerged in a mass of information but we do not know what to do with it. We try to store this information only to then forget about it, as it is washed over with another wave of information: the contents dies out for want of life after the information is received; and this is the main cause of the inefficiency of our office buildings.

At school, the same principle applies: the student will receive an education, much teaching, but only a small percentage of this will actually be useful. Why is there such a loss?

What the student does not communicate, he does not confront, he does not compare, and he does not share.

This is why our project is not a building but a CAMPUS; not an accumulation of sterile classrooms connected by functional corridors but a VILLAGE where all the spaces, the paths and the crossings are a pretext for encounters, discussion, adventure and the fruitful exchange of ideas. A place where a multitude of spaces and volumes, meetings of shadows, light and materials will allow the student to find his own place where he can adapt according to his own needs of action or gathering, of isolation or participation. And let the perspectives, the angles and the unusual views be generators of emotions and of FRUITFUL SURPRISES, in the creation not of a factory of artists but of a magma, an effervescence, a source of LIFE.

The student must have a very clear, emotional and memorable image of the school. He must be proud of belonging to it and working in it;

École des Beaux Arts, Paris
158 Perspectives and elevations

FACADE QUAI DE LA SEINE

FACADE QUAI DE LA LOIRE

École des Beaux Arts
159 Preliminary sketches

the usual subordinate relation of glass in respect of structural and architectural elements.

Only at night, through the power of artificial lighting, will the architecture of the interior – the arts and technical workshops, the amphitheatre, the library, the media library and the exhibition rooms, be fully visible: even the 'normality' of the daylight view is questioned and overturned.

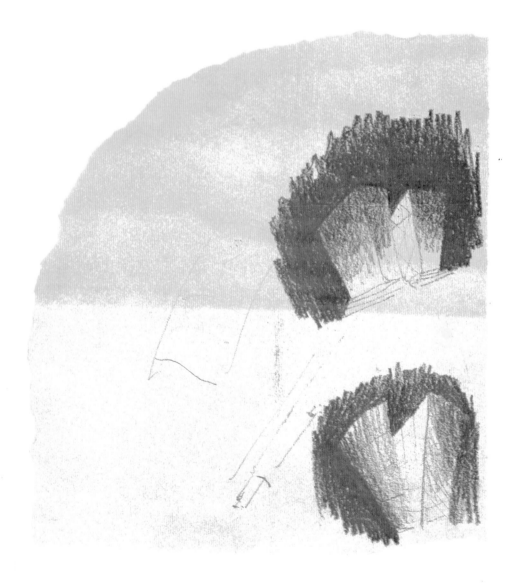

École des Beaux Arts, Paris
160 Preliminary sketches

but, in exchange, the emotional image must also be neutral, not even unconsciously dictating a style, not influencing the student in this way. The tool must be strong but open, UNSAID; and that is why we have chosen the strategy which is what we here at the office call the MEDUSA or rather the structured Medusa.

The building is an edifice without scale and relation to the real, put there as if by chance; an IMMATERIAL and undrawn response to the architecture of Ledoux. From the street, the passer-by cannot see a style or a particular type of architecture, but rather he can FEEL it. He can only feel the powerful energy, that effervescence animating the interior of these viscous blocks which, like Medusas and some transparent fish, allow their LIFE to be seen from without, palpitating and circulating in their multicoloured organs.

The school, then, sends out these unformulated messages towards the town of its formidable potential for passion and creativity. The town, in exchange, sends back its energy, its tension, its experience and its presence, but filtered down. This is why the school itself is TRANSLUCENT and not transparent.

Work is first of all a management of concentration and exploration of self; and, in accordance with this, although the school is 'permeable' it is not open towards the outside, but rather open to itself.

Its site means that the canal – a stretch of jade – slices this Pandora's box. And so much the

École des Beaux Arts, Paris
162 Preliminary drawing

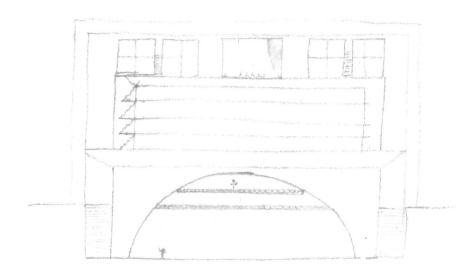

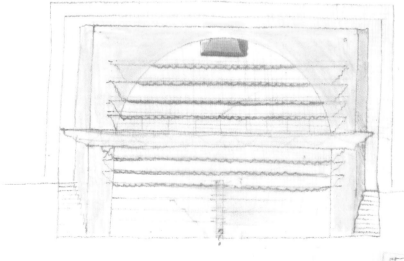

better; for it will be a pretext of exchange, challenges, demonstration and provocation – between it the school is transparent, communicative.

The building for the lower school is hollow, concave, open, a great empty arch waiting to fill itself with knowledge, that looks with envy towards the upper school, that Tower of Babel where already formed minds polish their knowledge and glorify their creativity. The passage from one part of the school to the other will be RITUALISED, each building projecting its bridge towards the other crystallising a unique and memorable moment. The bridge will then disappear to make way for historical perspective. The rest of the year it will be the foundation of the building and the canal which will act as a join between the lower and upper school, for, despite its exterior appearance, we are dealing with a single building whose submerged part is as important as its exposed part – for it is in these lower areas that COMMUNION takes place.

Schematically, at the top, we have a diversity of light for the teaching areas with classrooms making use both of lateral light and light from above; there are even roofs that open for the exhibition of sculptures in the open air.

In the middle we have administration areas.

At street level we have the very important communication with the surrounding area, its café, its shops, its galleries and the small hotel.

On the level below we have the public areas: auditoria, exhibition rooms, a library, and rooms for teaching audio-visual and virtual reality.

Then, finally, the great axis that passes between the buildings where the fantastic and surreal presence of the canal reigns which, transformed from contained to container, crosses the village square like an ocean liner.

KEY WORDS:
ENERGY
CAMPUS
COMMUNICATION
LIBERTY
EMOTION
TIMELESS
IMMATERIAL
UNSAID
SOUL

École des Beaux Arts, Paris
163 Preliminary drawing

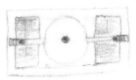

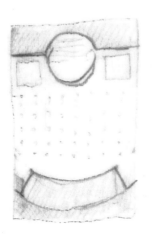

École des Beaux Arts, Paris
164 Preliminary drawing
165 Elevations, ground floor plan
and sections

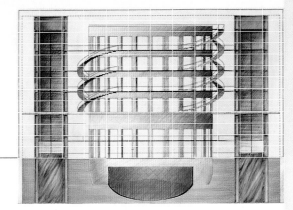

FACADE SUR LE CANAL DU BATIMENT QUAI DE LA LOIRE

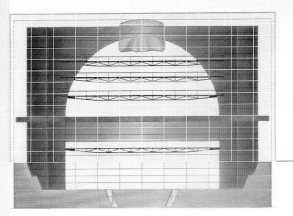

FACADE SUR LE CANAL DU BATIMENT QUAI DE LA SEINE

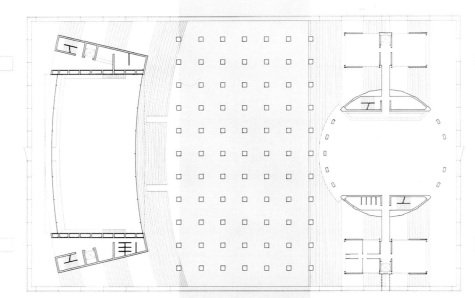

PLAN R.D.C. ET DE LA SALLE HYPOSTYLE

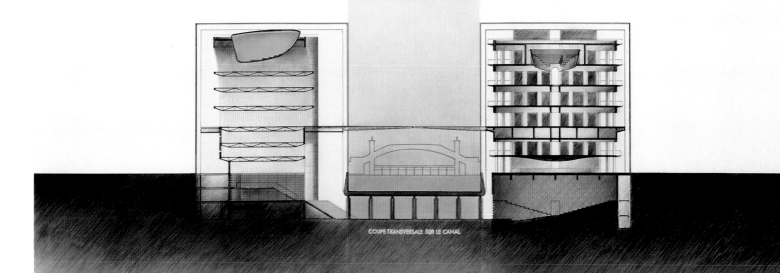

COUPE TRANSVERSALE SUR LE CANAL

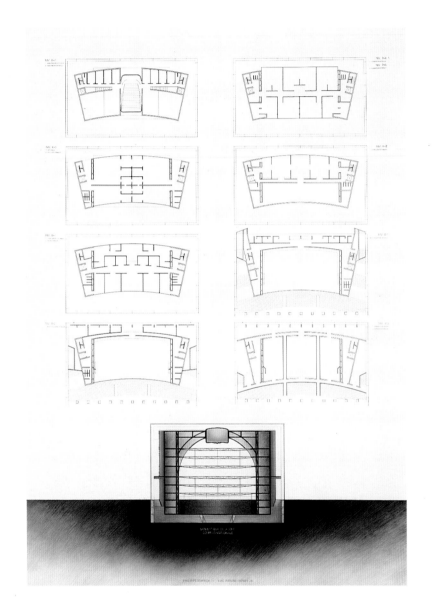

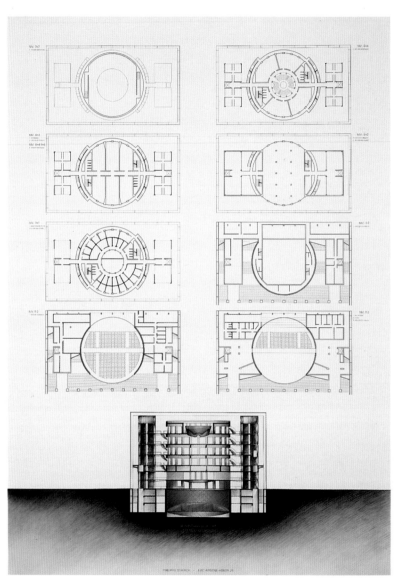

École des Beaux Arts, Paris
166 Plan and section of first building
167 Plan and section of second building

Project for Villa Placido Arango

Madrid, 1991

In the Arango house: the Mediterranean water house, a single window, the difficulty in locating the entrance, an improbable, De Chirico-inspired dwelling with closed arched doorways, the enclosing walls with three spires placed on top aligned with those of the house.

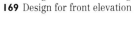

Villa Placido Arango, Madrid
168 Design of exterior arrangement
169 Design for front elevation

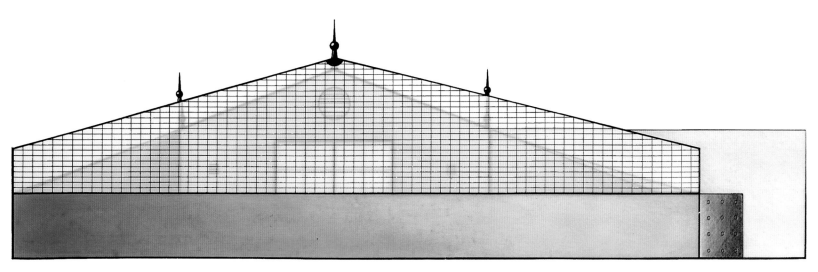

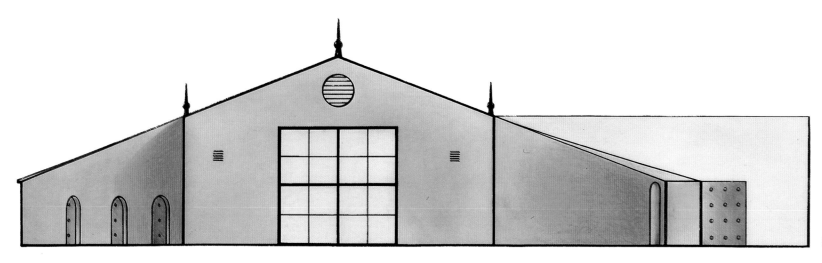

Museum of Modern Art Pavilion,
Groningen
170 Aerial perspective of overall scheme
by Alessandro Mendini (from *Elle Decor*,
October 1992)
171 Plan, section and elevation

Project for a Pavilion
Groningen Museum of Modern Art
Praediniussingel 59
Groningen, 1990-91

The main project for Groningen's Museum of Modern Art was realised by Alessandro Mendini's organisation, whilst the pavilions were undertaken by Frank Stella, Michele De Lucchi and Philippe Starck.

Starck's first project presents a circular edifice, sunk into the water on a square base, reminiscent of certain segregative typologies, such as pesthouses or defensive buildings – a fort or castle turret.

On the exterior, an imposing sloping black wall supports the cylindrical structure which is closed to the outside and destined for the exhibitions; in the interior, we find the upturned bottle-shaped pillars of the elevator, the stairwell, and services, and the serpentine progression of the exhibition elements.

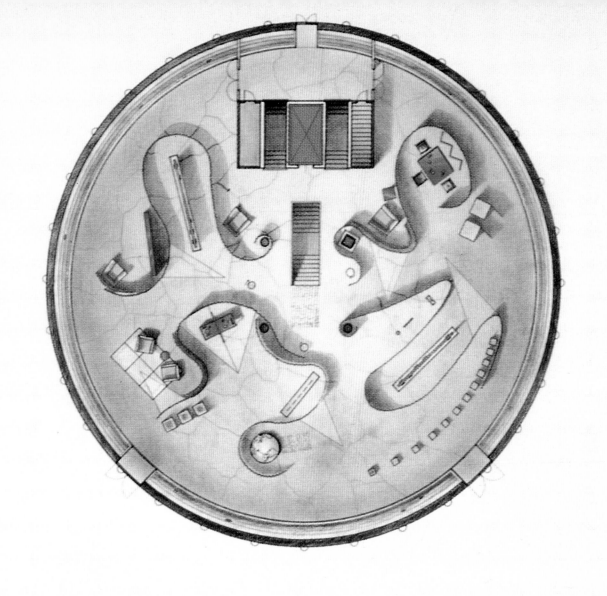

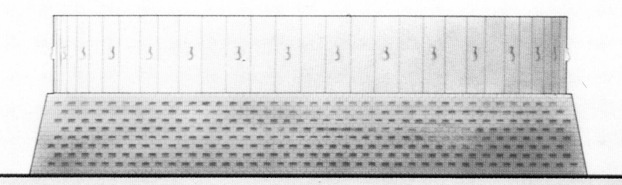

Hugo Boss Boutique

2 Place des Victoires

Paris, 1991

For Hugo Boss, mastery and soft tones: wall and ceiling boiserie, recurrent motifs in the veneers, door handles on the cabinets and windows, an opalescent bathroom with a corner mirror.

Hugo Boss Boutique, Paris
174 Detail of staircase
175 Staircase

'La rue Starck'

Rue Pierre Poli
Ile Saint Germain
Paris, 1991

Starck's plans for the arrangement of part of the Ile Saint Germain, where he has already built Maison Lemoult, are the only example, so far, of his vision of a city: an aggregation of autonomous and strong buildings, situated on a chequerboard symbolic of a virtual and metaphysical place.

Here Starck quotes himself, placing next to each other 'Nani Nani', Maison Lemoult, the project for his second house, 'The Angle' (in Antwerp) and other buildings, all of defensive appearance.

In the near future, according to Starck, the city 'will be a virtual city. A sort of non-city built on communications, which will reduce the movements of people and objects to the bare minimum. Just think of the fax. People will spend more and more time in their homes, and the home will be transformed into an electronic fort from which we will be able to transmit images and ideas anywhere. Computers, faxes and video-phones will drastically upset our habits, our lifestyles, our ways of working. The effect will be paradoxical.'

The totem-like and monumental buildings of 'La rue Starck' will be colonised by a new kind of humanity in which 'everyone will have a feeling of tremendous power, of being like a god. But the real masters will be elsewhere. The real masters will be the owners of the satellites and other means of communication. All it will take is for the owners to say: " . . . we're cutting you off" and you'll be forgotten by everyone. The violence of the future will not be through injuries, or death, it'll be through oblivion.'[1]

The scene described by Starck has apocalyptic overtones, but the catastrophe, although a realistic possibility, could be averted: 'It will be like living with the feet in the mud and the head in the sky. Everything will depend on us, on our imagination, on our capacity to adapt. It will be the end of the world or the beginning of the world.'[2]

In the cyberspace dominated by computers and virtual reality, Starck takes on the task, perhaps not of the hacker, but certainly of the cyberpunk: of someone who walks the razor edge between the diffusion of information and the challenging of the secretive handling of data.

'La rue Starck', Ile Saint Germain, Paris
176 Axonometric

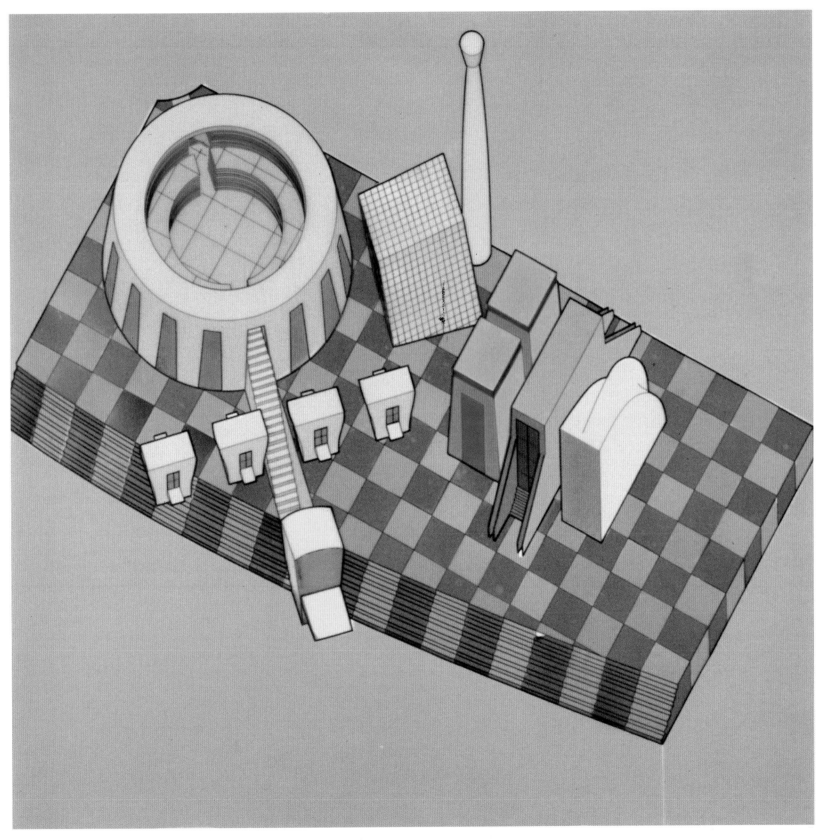

The sibylline questions of the cyberpunk attitude belong to Starck's ideological and formal vocabulary, like William Gibson he talks about the 'stroke': 'At the end of the twentieth century, the figure of the artist "stroke" ("/") scientist has become familiar. The cyberpunk, whether he fails or succeeds . . . [uses] the "stroke"'s attempt at communicating in both languages simultaneously. I think it is a very difficult task, sometimes impossible, but still worth trying.'[3]

1 Interview by M Di Forti with Philippe Starck in *Il Messaggero*, 4/6/1993
2 Ibid
3 'The William Gibson File' in *Decoder*, no 7, 1992

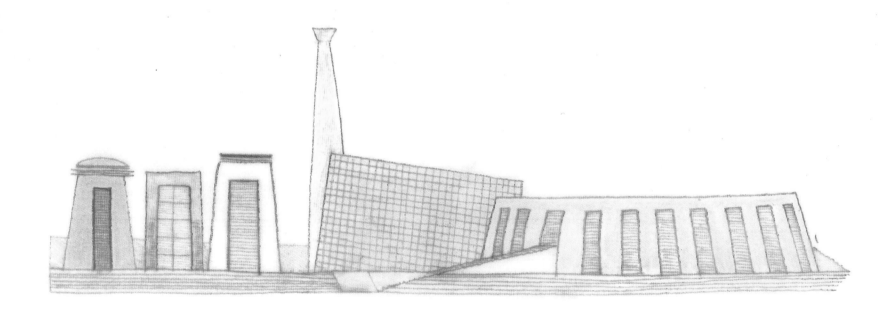

'La rue Starck', Ile Saint Germain, Paris
177 Preliminary drawing

'La rue Starck', Ile Saint Germain, Paris
178 Overall view

Project for Starck's Second House

27 Rue Pierre Poli
Ile Saint Germain
Paris, 1991

Having abandoned the design for the house in Montfort-L'Amaury,
Starck designed a second house for himself in Rue Poli in the Ile
Saint Germain. The front elevation has a single large window, and
a series of observatory-like box windows on the sloping side walls.
The means of access remain hidden and mysterious.

'The Angle'
16-17-18 Cockerillkaai
Antwerp, 1991

The front elevation of this multipurpose building suggests an imbalanced structure, inclined to one side as if the foundations were giving way. This is underlined by the four arched doorways at the base which contrast with the front window section which is perpendicular to the ground, as if the weaker core of the interiors had resisted the collapse of the main structure.

'The Angle', Antwerp
180 Drawing
181 Project for front elevation

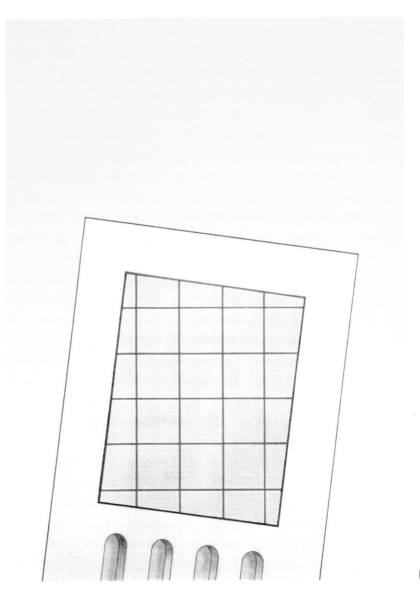

474 and 6 Cubes
Projects for Residence Buildings 474 and 204
South Venice Boulevard
Venice, California, 1992

Two exercises on the object which can be both a piece of furniture and become architecture as well. For Starck it's only a matter of scale. '474', a military hangar that doesn't reveal 'secret' activities; '6 Cubes', a glass fronted cabinet with doors, complete with knobs, but placed on the inside.

Toar
Project for Two Buildings in the Parc de Bercy

Paris, 1992

Commissioned by the Compagnie du Parc de Bercy, Starck proposed two twin buildings, reminiscent of the 'terribleness' of certain paleo-industrial buildings, and the era of the glorification of the machine.

Starck summarises examples of Antonio Saint' Elia, standard-bearer of the futuristic glorification of the 'modern times' (the bodies of the elevators and the vertical connections placed around the buildings and connected to them by external balconies, and the oblique development of the walls), of Mendelsohn (curved glass sections and observatory-style opening dome), and of certain 'bolidist' architectural styles, derived from the world of comics.

The two buildings rest on a chequered area, a constant reminder of the ubiquity of the place, and have a rectangular structure with semicircular extremities. There are three elevations: a sloping base with a series of tall and narrow pillars, reminiscent of 'Nani Nani'; a central section with glass panels lined with balconies; and a domed top which in its minor aspects alludes to the typology of light houses or observatories.

The best view of the building is certainly at night, as suggested by the design's rendering, which emphasises the vertical glass sections of the base, and the horizontal ones of the subsequent five floors which culminate in the dome's aperture out of which comes the great beam of light probing the skies and the urban landscape.

Toar, Paris
184 Preliminary sketch for terraces

199

Toar, Paris
185 Preliminary design
for elevations
186 Elevations

TOAR • 1992

Toar, Paris
187 Preliminary overall design
188 Overall perspective

Toar, Paris
189 Elevation of inside wall
190 Elevation of outside wall

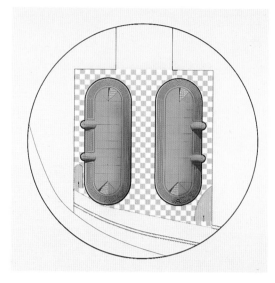

Toar, Paris
191 Roof plan

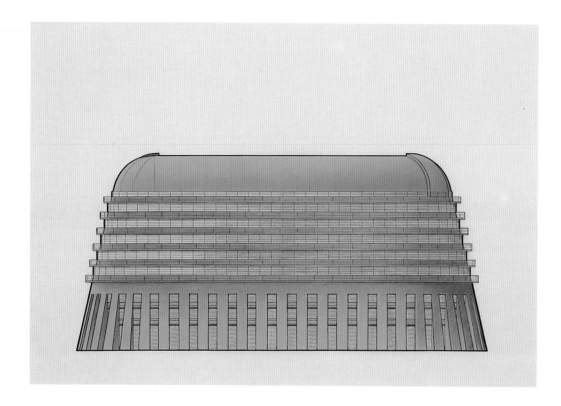

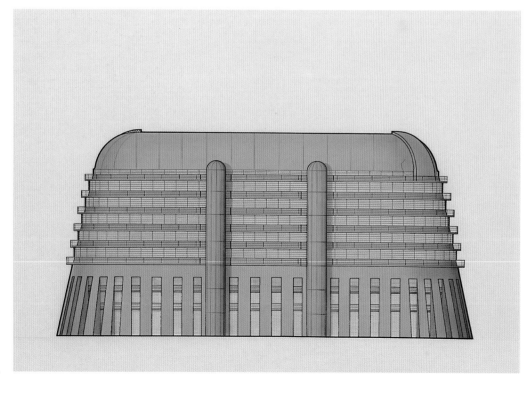

Toar, Paris
192 Overall elevations, roof plan and detail

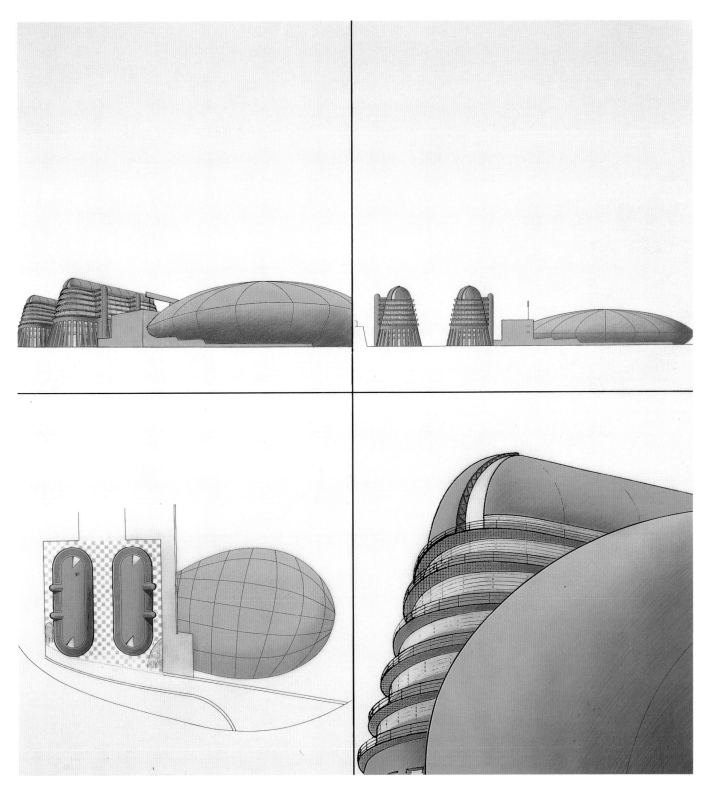

Street furniture, JC Decaux
193 Traffic lights
194 Waste disposal unit
195 Overall view of various elements

Project for Elements of Street Furniture
JC Decaux

1990-92

Typical aspects of Starck's activity as a designer converge in this project for elements of street furniture commissioned by the Decaux company. Before this, the same theme had been tackled in furnishing the Parc de La Villette in Paris, and had been resolved with a tubular vertical element into which a series of signals with a teardrop section were progressively inserted. In the project for Decaux, the modular hypothesis is dropped in favour of a stronger and almost totem-like presence: from the waste bins with the appearance of domestic robots to the traffic lights with the threatening pointed pole, from the anthropomorphic benches to the illumination poles, almost like bone articulations.

For Starck, everything has to become a communicative object and has to invoke attention and reflection: even the most typical symbols of an alienating life.

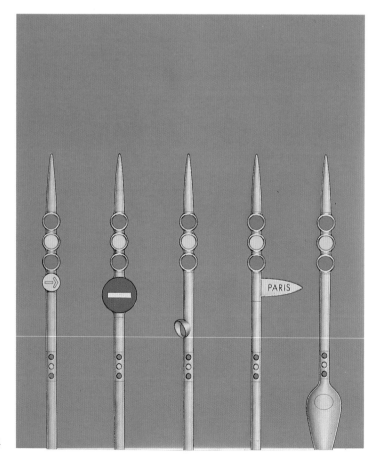

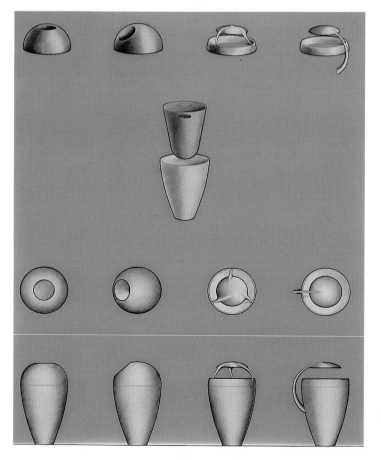

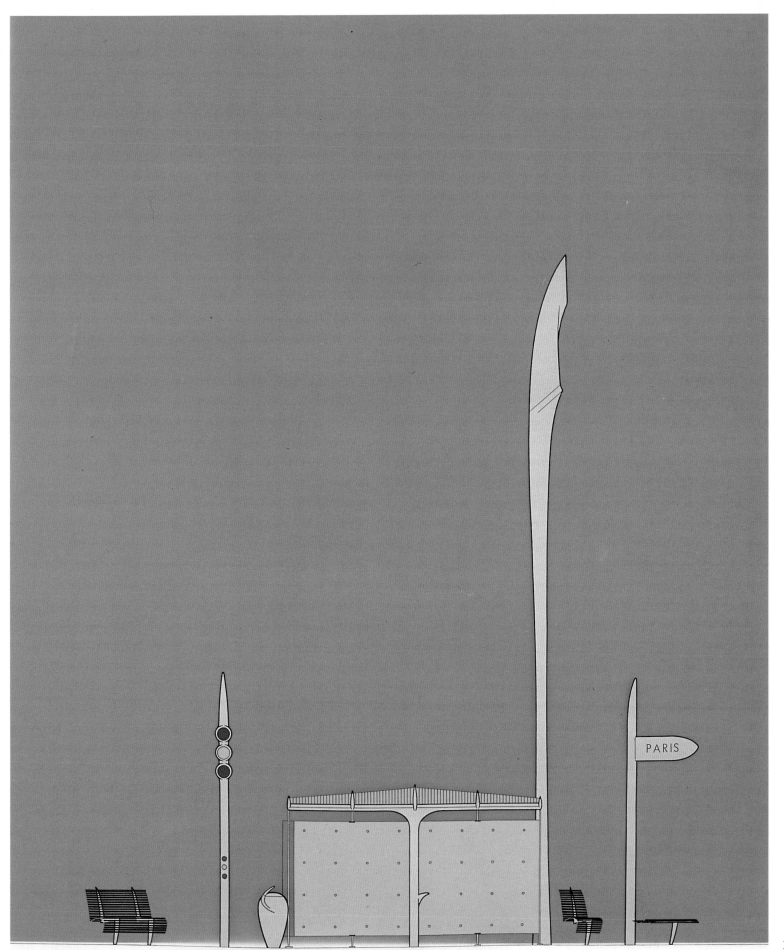

Street furniture, JC Decaux
196 Designs for lighting elements
197 Designs for lighting elements

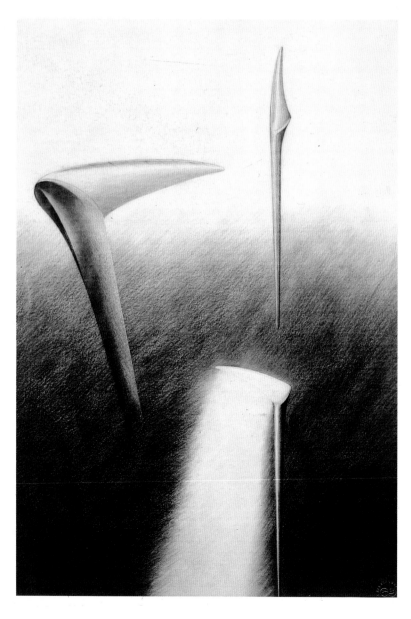

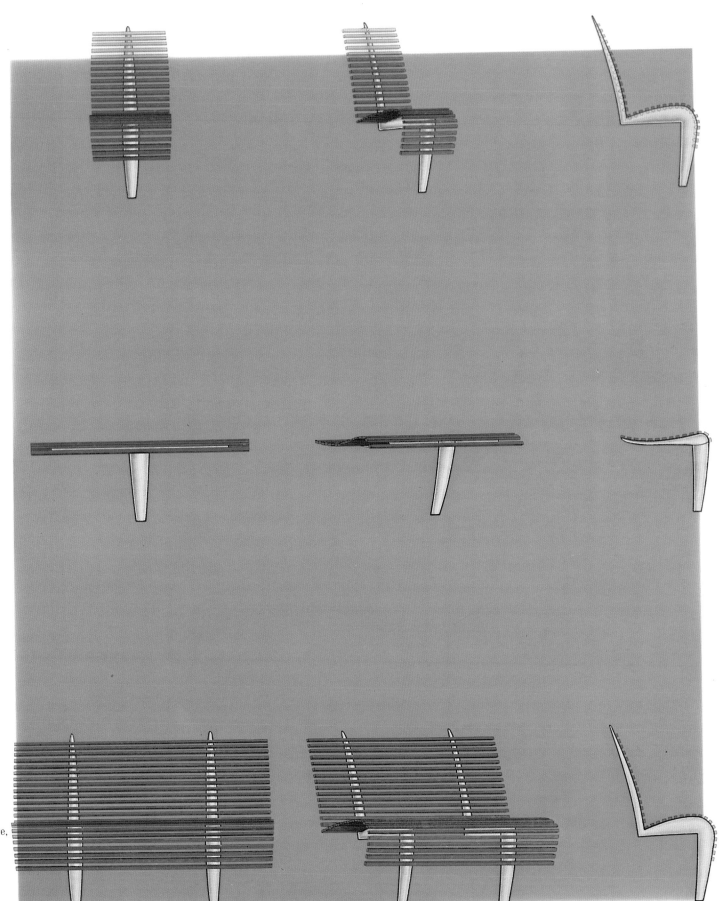

Street furniture,
JC Decaux
198 Benches

Project for the École Nationale Supérieure des Arts Décoratifs

(Competition entry in collaboration with Luc Arsène-Henry jr)
Rue d'Ulm
Paris, 1992

In the project for the ENSAD, Starck faces for the first time the theme of relations and confrontations between pre-existing elements in the European city. His method does not change: to introduce a foreign body.

The historic school building on the Rue d'Ulm is preserved and keeps its function of access, whilst the corner building is converted. On the Rue d'Erasme a new building is introduced, characterised by a great drape-like opalescent glass front bordered at the bottom by a moulded bronze element. The corner of this building appears to have been clawed at. The surprise effect introduced by the new building is very apparent: a sort of paradoxical enlargement, an absurd disproportioning of a small precious box.

From the traditional style entrance, one moves, via a first room with an elevated floor which follows the shape of a dolphin's back, through to the vestibule which gives access to the terrace, to the garden with the Vissol tempietto, and to the school. The side of the new building facing the garden is slanted, and particular attention is paid to both its interiors (such as the partially glazed walls, a model of Le Corbusierian inspiration, which at the same time separate and connect the classrooms and the corridors), and the exteriors, like the grilles at the foot of the trees that curve surrealistly to include the neighbouring garden, or the benches shaped to protect the entire trunk of the trees. The characteristic element of the intervention has to be the great undulating glass front tinted with a pale opalescent green which, like a filter, allows one to perceive, but not to see directly, the life within the school.

As in the design for the École des Beaux Arts, the glass front has the double role of uniting and separating, seeing and not seeing, according to a spirit that never accepts the usual and consolidated rules, but on the contrary is always willing to break the mould in search of new possibilities, a new vision, new ways of life.

The École Nationale Supérieure des Arts Décoratifs building is indeed 'decorative'.

Like a decorated whale on the verge of extinction, the school evokes memories, feelings that transport you to another plane where the eye is pleasantly surprised, is amused and interested in the language of a particular motif, the magic of a reflection, the premeditation of a bridge. This building, with its rich and varied material, will be an example of another creative way forward.

Let us see what the building can tell us as we wander through the space of the École.

The mosaic of the facades has been kept intact, reminding us of the almost human evolution of the school through time. The first historic building in the Rue d'Ulm has been maintained in its original state. This building can be seen as the beginning, the base; modernity will come from elsewhere. The corner building has been restyled; and the elements that were making it age prematurely, for example the curtain facade and its excess aluminium, have now been replaced by glazing that forms an ephemeral screen.

The new Erasmus building will balance the centimetric vision of its opaline screen, undulating creamy-light curtains and pipes of wrought bronze. And, with its overgrown toy-like scale, the building will signify play and emotion.

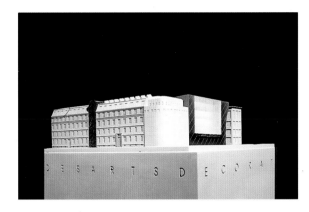

École Nationale Supérieure
des Arts Décoratifs, Paris
199 Model, view of the corner at the Rue d'Ulm and Rue d'Erasme
200 Model, view of the facade on the Rue d'Erasme

École Nationale Supérieure
des Arts Décoratifs, Paris
201 Courtyard corner

Let us now open the door that retains all its original features: behind it, however, a curved floor will indicate that times have indeed changed. This 'bridge' leads us to an aisle through a luminescent terrace – a place for wandering, meetings and conversations. Here we come to the garden.

Making our way towards the school and noticing, at this point, the exhibition space through the arcade, we now come to the centre of gravity, the 'knot' formed by the three corners of the three buildings – a curved, oblique break through which will flow all the life of the school, spreading out on to the great spiral stair in concrete brick, the bronze footbridges, and the openings of the two facades which are open like a book.

The school has to be understood in its entirety – faced head on, challenged and enriched.

Light shines through large bronze grilles, through the pale green cracks – concentrated pearls of wisdom. Elsewhere, light filters through dreamily, enigmatically – an all-encompassing sheen, reflecting the global vision of the school.

On the various floors, the walls are never truly open and never fully closed, with their glass partitions, frosted glass walls, wooden screens, light and heavy curtains allowing both full and fragmented views – perhaps of a passer-by or a corner of a drawing, a glimpse of colour on a design.

Having been welcomed into this space, everyone lives together at the heart of a lively group.

The furniture is seen as a set of tools positioned in a workspace, in a solid, classical, intemporal base, welcoming a variety of responses. Now at the end of our stroll through this space, we come to the garden and to 'Vissol', that small crystal cube, a tiny temple of love where our university students can meet our artists.
Peaceful contemplation
Joy
Creativity

AXONOMETRIE SUR ESCALIER ANGLE/ERASME

HALL D'ENTREE

GRILLE D'ARBRE

BANC DE JARDIN

RANGEMENT ETUDIANTS

CLOISON SEMI-VITREE

École Nationale
Supérieure des
Arts Décoratifs,
Paris
202 Details

211

École Nationale Supérieure
des Arts Décoratifs, Paris
203 Preliminary sketches

ÉCOLE NATIONALE SUPÉRIEURE DES ARTS DÉCORATIFS • 1992

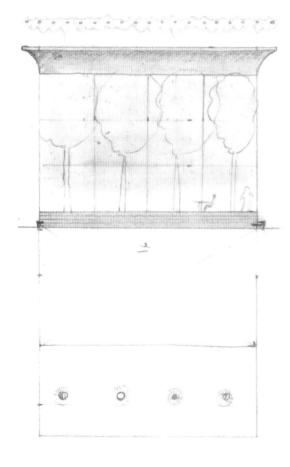

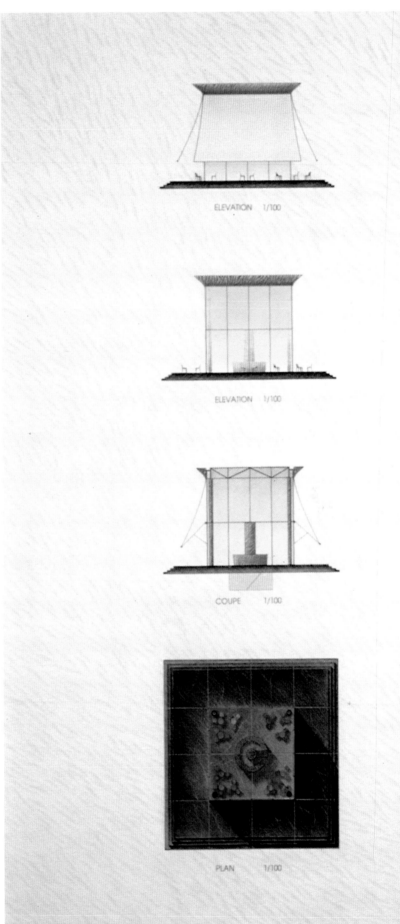

ELEVATION 1/100

ELEVATION 1/100

COUPE 1/100

PLAN 1/100

École Nationale Supérieure
des Arts Décoratifs, Paris
204 Preliminary drawings
for the Vissol 'tempietto'
205 Designs for the Vissol 'tempietto'

213

École Nationale Supérieure
des Arts Décoratifs, Paris
206 Section and facade facing rue d'Erasme
207 Section and side of new building

École Nationale Supérieure
des Arts Décoratifs, Paris
208 Plan

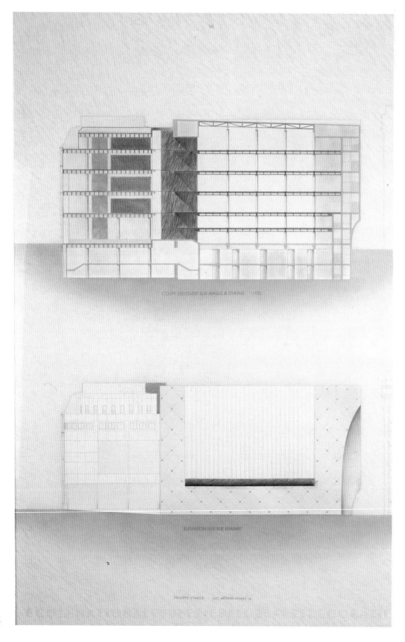

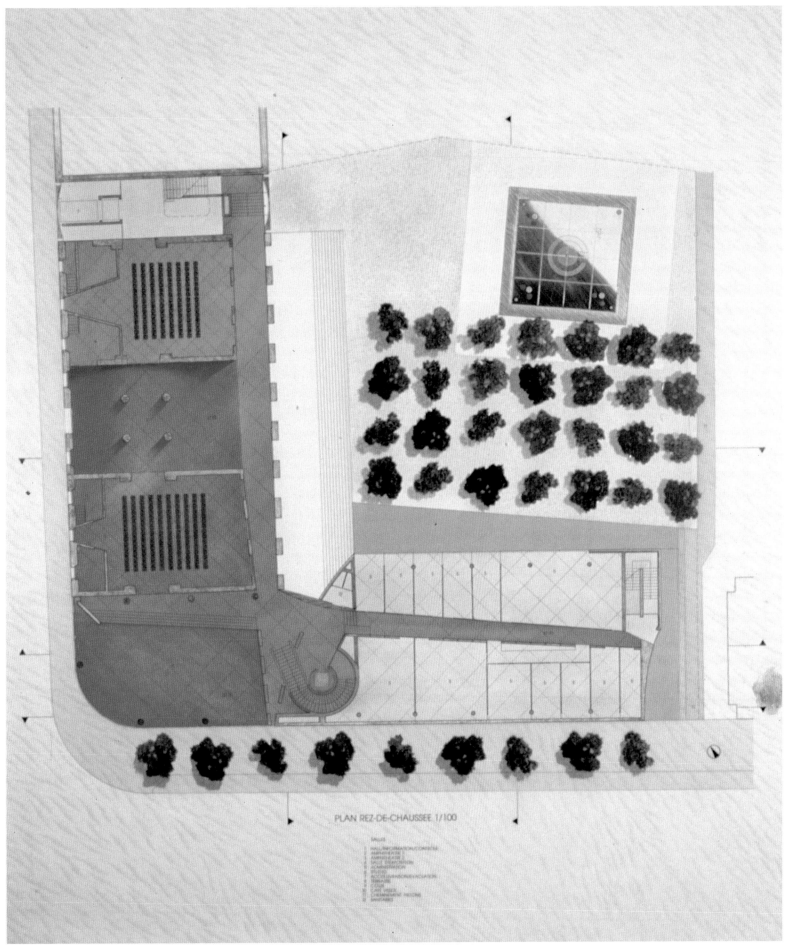

PLAN REZ-DE-CHAUSSEE 1/100

Project for Control Tower
Bordeaux-Merignac Airport
(In collaboration with Luc Arsène-Henry jr)
1993

In the text that accompanies the project, Starck cannot avoid referring to the influence of the designs of his father, an aeronautical engineer, and underlining the unique affinity between the control tower and the aerodynamic forms of the planes.

Various possible ideas emerge from the preliminary sketches: from the theme of the entrance translated into the almost anthropomorphic portal structure, to the solutions of inclined and deformed cylinders, (amongst which the tower stands out, partly covered with glass and following the course of the staircase to the cylinder, flattened at the top to accommodate the terrace). It is this interest in deformation, typical of Starck, which makes the geometrical forms assume connotations that are not structural or geometrically abstract, but more properly symbolic and semantic. In other words, the tower is intended as an element which is not only functional but also, above all, whose strongly significant presence is impossible to ignore. The final design is materialised in a structure that opens at the top with an upturned, eliptical cross-sectioned cylinder, attached by means of diagonal cuts, similar to those experimented with on the project for 'Le Baron Vert'.

The reference to aeronautics is indicated by the eliptical section of the tower, by the out-of-axis terrace with jutting parapets, by the complex of the control room and the inclined progress of the walkways.

Guardian Angel
As a young boy, my bed used to be underneath my father's drawing board. At night, I used to lie amongst my father's things: empty glasses, compasses and slide rules. The wallpaper around me was of aircraft tails and outlines of wings with their skilfully designed and elegant lines. I was born in the sky and grew up by the airfields; and now, as a learner pilot, I am still living there. So today I would like to bring this intuitive sense of flying to fruition, renew my ties so to speak, and, above all, to attempt to bring my own small contribution to join the live adventure of French aeronautics, in which my father was one of the humble players. I owe everything to the spirit and genius of French engineering; and now I would like to show it my thanks. I lived respecting the control tower, one of the most powerful symbols of aviation. The control tower is the all-protecting and welcoming eye; it is the indispensable element to flying and to landing. This powerful sign is no ordinary sign; through its necessity and modernity it is devoted to being an emblem, a bearer of all the dreams that have made men want to fly.

We hope that we have been able to respond to the numerous questions put forward by the vital and complex functions of this control tower.

It is normal, it is deserved.

There are others who will see to adding everything to the building that it needs to keep running properly; making sure that it is well ventilated, well looked after.

It is normal, it is deserved.

The construction and the upkeep now taken care of, we also have to think of the people without whom all this would only be a pile of scrap iron: the air-traffic controllers.

I have the impression that elsewhere they would be seen as red-eyed extensions of a dominating screen.

Our choice, however, was the human being, his life and his happiness.

At the heart of our project lies the notion of a place that is free and open, and which, from the terrace to the watchtower, passing through the main room, will create work at its optimum level, and the calm and rest in order to best achieve that – participating in, communicating and taking pleasure in this work. A place of energy and dreams, 46 metres from the ground.

When the essence of a project has been found, everything else becomes easy and flows, just like this pure, essential tower, modelled on the image, the strength and the materials of the planes that it controls.

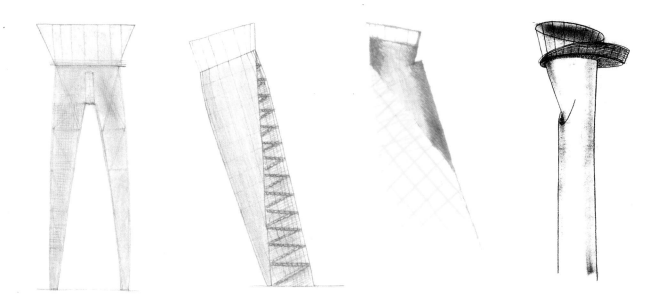

Control Tower,
Bordeaux-Merignac Airport
209 Preliminary sketches
210 Plans, sections and elevations

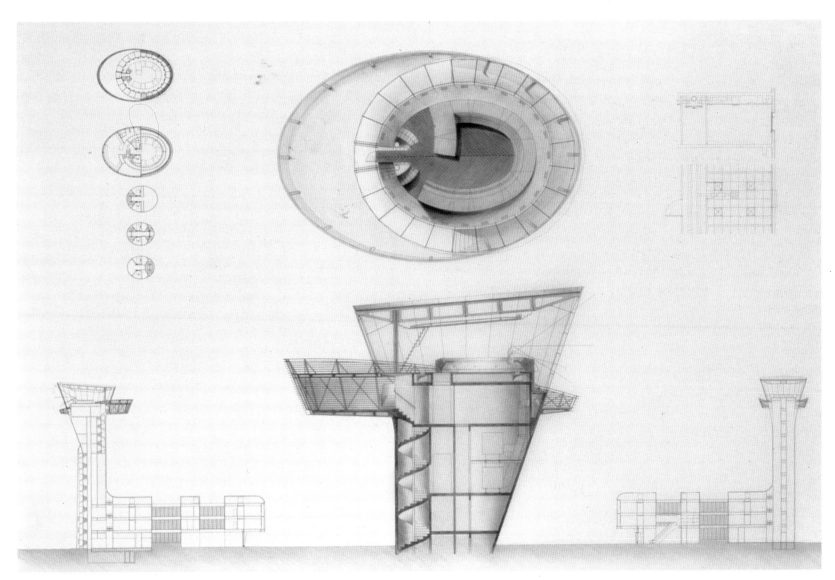

Prefabricated House for '3 Suisses'

1993

In 1993, when referring to the press releases on his early ideas for a prefabricated house for '3 Suisses', Starck hinted at the hypothesis of an economical house, to be purchased by catalogue and constructed by a company internationally renowned for the production and distribution of furnishings. In the early, brief announcements Starck also mentioned the possibility, for the buyer, of including variations (location of dividing walls, windows, etc) that would allow for the personalisation of the finished product. A Starck house then, to be mail-ordered like any other furnishing element or object, removing the usual bureaucratic and technical rituals.

The prototype relates to what Starck has said concerning the dichotomy between his public and private architecture: whilst in the former the dominant factors are the communicative (semantic) element and a design process moving from the exterior to the interior, in the latter it is the importance of the interior that is highlighted (and as a consequence the exterior is merely its resolution), and the attention to comforts. 'Private architecture . . . goes from the inside to the outside; in other words, here I'm only interested in art, culture, semantics; here I'm only interested in the small qualities of life, the small comforts, the private, happy moment . . . the nice kitchen that brightens up when you're having breakfast, the proximity of the bathroom, the log fire: essentially the small-scale comforts.'

Starck's prefabricated house is really an updated version of a blend of the old American standard 'balloon frame' technique of wood constructions and the typology of the garden pavilion of vaguely Oriental inspiration.

The use of humble materials such as the bare wooden planks of the steps, the varnished wood of the interiors, the metal sheets of the roof, the glass and the rough-hewn trunks of the portico (the use of the 'rustic' style is intelligent, refined and ironic) is congenial both to the demands for economy and the pre-existing standards of building practices. However, there remains a certain degree of monumentality in this small building (the steps, the symmetry, the portico, the double order of the pagoda-style roof) which, although translated through the use of 'humble' materials, still manages to confer a sense of privilege to the building and its immediate sur-

roundings.

Prefabricated House
for '3 Suisses'
211 Detail of roofing
212 Detail of access steps
213 Exterior

Probing again in the collective subconscious, Starck has produced the timeless wooden house in the woods, isolated, welcoming, rich in its interiors of objects and affections; the house that, sooner or later, we all dream of.

Prefabricated House
for '3 Suisses'
214 Interior
215 Interior
216 Interior

AWARDS

1980
'Oscar du Luminaire' for the 'Easylight' lamp.
Laureate of the International Competition for the Lecture
Rooms at the Science Museum in the Parc de La Villette,
Paris.
Laureate of the International Competition for Urban
Furniture at the Parc de la Villette.

1985
'Créateur de l'Année'

1986
Neocone of Chicago, awarded three prizes for furniture
'Delta de Plaia', Barcelona.
Winner at the New York Chair Fair with the 'Costes' chair.

1987
'Platinum Circle Award' for Café Costes, Chicago.
Prize for the 'Ray Hollis' ashtray, Tokyo.
Prize for the 'J Lang' chair.

1988
'Grand Prix National de la Création Industrielle'.
'Oscar du Design' for the Beneteau boat.

1990
'100 Design' editorial award, USA.
'1990 Interior Design Award – Hall of Fame' for the
Royalton Hotel, New York.

1991
'Twelfth Annual Interiors Awards' for his hotels, New York
'AIA Honour Award' for his hotels, Washington.
'1991 Interior Design Award – Hall of Fame' for the
Paramount Hotel, New York.

1992
First nomination from the Brooklyn Museum for
'Outstanding Achievement in Contemporary Design', New
York.
Member of the 'Centre National des Arts Plasitques',
Ministry of Culture, France.
Teacher at the Domus Academy, Milan.
Teacher at the Decorative Arts School, Paris.
Art Director for the 'International Design Yearbook' for one
year, UK.
'Chevalier des Arts et des Lettres'.
'Officier des Arts et des Lettres'.
'1992 Honour Award' for the Paramount Hotel, awarded by
the American Institute of Architects.

1993
'Top Ten' upholstered furniture design award (Europe), for
chairs produced for Driade, Germany.

EXHIBITIONS

1985
Centre Georges Pompidou, 'Nouveaux Plaisirs d'Architecture'
Museum of French Monuments, Paris, 'Art et Industrie'
Museum of Modern Art, Kyoto, Japan; Seibu, Tokyo, Japan

1986
Centre Georges Pompidou, 'Créer dans le Crée'
Kunstmuseum, Düsseldorf, 'Emotional Collages'
Stuttgart Erkundungen, International Design Congress
Frankfurt, Germany, 'Letein 3'
Neocone 18, Chicago
Los Angeles, 'Modern Props'

1987
Centre Georges Pompidou, 'Nouvelles Tendances'
Boulogne, France, 'Les Cent Chaises'
Marseilles, France, 'Starck Mobilier'
Maison Descartes, Amsterdam, 'Vice Versa'
Munchen Deutsch Museum, 'International Glass Design Work'

1988
Centre Georges Pompidou, 'Thirty Years of French Design'

1989
Palais des Beaux Arts de Charleroi

1990
Museum of Decorative Arts, Paris; Venice Biennale

1992
Hochschule Museum, Vienna 'Starck in Vienna'

1993
MUKHA Museum, Anvers, 'Starck Architecture'
Design Museum, London 'Starck in London'
Le Grand Palais, Paris 'Design Miroir du Siècle'

1994/95
Centre Georges Pompidou, Starck exhibition

PERMANENT STARCK COLLECTIONS

Decorative Arts Museum, Paris • Brooklyn Museum, New
York • Design Museum, London • Centre Georges
Pompidou, Paris • Vitra Design Museum, Switzerland

BIBLIOGRAPHY

Within the extremely vast bibliography concerning Starck's activity the following titles must be highlighted as the main contributions:

1987   M Aveline, *Philippe Starck, Mobilier 1970-87*, Marseilles
1989   C Colin, *Starck*, Liège-Milano
1991   *Starck*, a cura di O Boissière, Köln
1992   F Irace, *Dimore metropolitane*, Milano

Whilst the first publication deals mainly with Starck's activity as designer, the others mention his architectural production in addition to vast bibliographies.

Of the newspaper and magazine articles on Starck, those which deal with his architecture and interior design are listed here.

1983   M Champenois, 'Les Habits neufs de L'Elysée', *Le Monde* (France)
1985   M Breitmann, 'Philippe Starck, Designer-Architecte', *AMC* (Germany)
        C Clifford, 'Café Costes', *The World of Interiors* (USA)
        L Dispot, 'Le triomphe du Café Costes', *Pariscope* (France)
        F Edelmann, 'Café Costes, la mode s'y retrouve', *Le Monde* (France)
        B Fitoussi, 'Philippe Starck', *L'Architecture d'Aujourd'hui* (France)

1986   S Slesin, 'Parisian Café Celebrates the Melancholy', *The New York Times* (USA)
        'Mobilier urbain', *Architecture Intérieure Créé* (France)
        'Concours international pour le mobilier urbain du parc de la Villette', *L'Architecture d'Aujourd'hui* (France)

1987   F Baudot, 'Starck à Tokyo', *Décoration Internationale* (France)
        'Architecture Wonderland, Philippe Starck', *Styling* (Japan)
        'Out Tonight – Manin Tokyo', *Architecture Intérieure Créé* (France)

1988   Y Kageyama, 'Designer Starck into "Mystiques"', *The Japan Times Weekly* (Japan)

1989   'Echt Starck: Das Royalton', *Ambiente* (Germany)
        J Burt, 'The Hippest Hotel in Manhattan', *Blueprint* (UK)

C Colin, 'The Royalton', *Galeries Magazine* (France)
D Gomez-Vallarcel, 'Super Starck Hotel', *Casa Vogue* (Spain)

1990   F Baudot, 'Le Paramount à New York, Starck persiste et signe', *Elle* (France)
        F Chaslin, 'Biennale de Venise', *L'Architecture d'Aujourd'hui* (France)
        C Colin, 'L'Emprise des Signes, Paramount Hotel', *Architecture Intérieur Créé* (France)
        C Colin, 'Teatriz Olé', *Architecture Intérieure Créé* (France)
        R Doerk, B Knauf, 'Paramount', *Ambiente* (Germany)
        B Friedrich, 'Super Starck in Tokyo', *Architektur & Wohnen* (Germany)
        KS Leuschtel, '"Teatriz" oder die Inszenierung des Gastes', *Hochparterre* (Switzerland)
        P Popham, 'Starck in Tokyo: Paper-weight Architecture', *Blueprint* (UK)
        JP Robert, 'Le Nani Nani de Starck', *L'Architecture d'Aujourd'hui* (France)
        M Romanelli, 'Philippe Starck, architetture a Tokyo tra il 1987 e il 1990', *Domus* (Italy)
        'Teatriz', *Ambiente* (Germany)
        'Fuego y piedra, Starck en Tokyo', *Ardi* (Spain)
        'Wim Wenders Office by Starck', *Ambiente Spezial* (Germany)

1991   P Castro, 'El Hotel Paramount', *Diseño Interior* (Spain)
        B Fitoussi, 'Paramount Hotel New York', *L'Architecture d'Aujourd'hui* (France)
        S Walther Mathieu, 'Home Away From Home', *Atrium* (Germany)
        M Serrano Marzo, 'El Teatro Teatriz de Philippe Starck', *On Diseño* (Spain)
        F Premon, 'A New York. Firmato Philippe Starck', *Casa Vogue* (Italy)
        'Ein Franzose in New York', *Schöner Wohnen* (Germany)
        'Philippe Starck', *Interior Design* (USA)
        'Annual Luce 1991-92, realtà e magia', from an interview between V Pasca and Philippe Starck, *Disegnare la dematerializzazione*